CHAPTERS

Introduction
1. Your Incredible Brain   5
2. The Basis of Memory   29
3. Improving Memory   41
4. Memory Aids   57
5. The Power of your Imagination   75
6. The Genesis of Accelerated Learning   87
7. What is the Role of the Music?   97
8. The Evidence   111
9. Tell Me   131
10. The State of the Art   149
11. Putting it All Together   165
12. First - Relax   177
13. An Accelerated Learning Course   187
14. Accelerated Learning for your Children   209
15. How You can be Involved   215
16. Notes for Teachers   217

ACCELERATED LEARNING

Colin Rose

Accelerated Learning Systems Limited
England

Colin Rose is a graduate of London University and a member of the British Association for the Advancement of Science. He has researched and reported on several previous major developments that have broken new scientific ground.

First Published in Great Britain 1985
Second Edition September 1986
Third Edition Published April 1988
Fourth Edition June 1989
Fifth Edition July 1991
by Accelerated Learning Systems Ltd.,
50 Aylesbury Road, Aston Clinton, Aylesbury, Bucks.

© Colin Rose 1985

Reprinted March 1992

ISBN 0 905553 128

Typeset by Graham Jeffery Creative Services — Aylesbury, Bucks.
Front Cover by Philip Giggle
Printed by Clays Ltd, St Ives plc

INTRODUCTION

A quiet revolution is gathering momentum in the way we learn. In the last decade or so psychologists have begun to discover more of how the brain really works and how facts can be rapidly and deeply fixed in the memory. It's on these discoveries that Accelerated Learning is based.

Historically, most teaching has been undertaken by those who were the best at the subject - the person who was "best at French", became the French teacher. But that person was not necessarily the most skilled at the principles of teaching. You employ an architect to design your house, because his speciality is the principle of construction but a builder to actually carry out the plans, because he is adept at the practice.

In a similar way psychologists have begun to define the principles behind learning, and these findings have led to a quite different approach to learning.

Conventional teaching has assumed that learning should involve determined concentration and frequent repetition. We now know that this style of learning is not efficient, because it causes unnecessary tension and it tends to involve just one half of the brain.

Accelerated Learning, in contrast, teaches you how to achieve a pleasantly relaxed, yet receptive state of mind, and presents information in new ways that actively involve both the left and right brains.

There can be no learning without memory. We remember things easily that have powerful associations for us - which is why T.V. advertisers use strong visual images, use music and rhythm, and attempt to involve our emotions. It's the reason why you can remember the words of a pop song with little or no conscious effort, yet struggle to remember a list of historical dates.

By studying why people can remember some things vividly after a single exposure, yet forget other information after dozens of repetitions, we have been able to construct new techniques of teaching. They create such powerful associations that pupils find they can literally picture what they are learning in their "mind's eye" and hear what they are learning in their "mind's ear". The methods have been evolved from studies on people with photographic memory.

Accelerated Learning, however, does not only work by setting up memorable visual and sound associations in the mind. A high proportion of all learning takes place at the subconscious level. So Accelerated Learning presents the student with new material in such a way that it is simultaneously absorbed by both the conscious and subconscious mind. Information, for example, is positioned so it can be absorbed in peripheral vision, and sentences are short and rhythmical because such facts are easily remembered.

The attraction, and paradox, is that the learner puts in no more conscious effort than normal; in fact less because she or he is relaxed. It is the fact that the material is presented in such a memorable way, to both the left and right brains, and to the conscious and subconscious mind, that accounts for the dramatic improvement in the speed and effectiveness of learning.

Accelerated Learning is not the development of one man. Dozens of Universities, Research Psychologists and professional educators have contributed to produce this unique way of presenting new information. The contributions range from the seminal work of Dr. Lozanov, to Nobel Prize winners Roger Sperry and Robert Ornstein, and to the recent work of N.L.P. researchers.

There are Accelerated Learning courses now in scores of Universities around the world. The technique has been incorporated in the Finnish school system by many individual teachers and also in the school system of the city of Chicago. Multi-national companies such as Shell Oil, General Motors and Hilton Hotels are using the method - as are dozens of U.S. Government Agencies and Embassies.

The effectiveness of Accelerated Learning has been objectively measured and Don Schuster, Professor of Psychology at Iowa State University, was able to record that *"it produces at least 300% improvement in the speed and effectiveness of learning"*.

This book presents the background to the development of Accelerated Learning, the evidence, and describes the methods step by step. You will be able to try the technique and prove it for yourself.

We believe the impact of Accelerated Learning will be felt in every area of learning. UNESCO have acknowledged its effectiveness in learning languages, and the magazine "Educational Technology" claimed that *"it is a tool that allows students to absorb and retain a two year language course in as few as 20 days. Almost any factual subject matter - chemistry, financial, medical, even management sciences can be presented in this framework. It is destined to have a revolutionary impact on human resources in the days to come"*.

"Psychology" magazine called Accelerated Learning *"The key to the 21st Century"* and Educational Psychologist Dr. Jean Houston claims *"we are just beginning to discover the virtually limitless capacities of the mind"*.

Certainly it is a timely breakthrough, because we live in an age where the fast acquisition of more and more knowledge is a necessity. Accelerated Learning can achieve this, and because the results are so immediate, learning becomes enjoyable, satisfying and therefore motivating.

YOUR INCREDIBLE BRAIN

The recent discoveries in Inner Space

The human brain appears over-endowed. It used to be an often quoted statistic that we only use 10% of our potential brain power. The more psychologists have learnt in the last ten years however, the less likely they are to dare to attempt to quantify our brain potential. The only consistent conclusion is that the proportion of our potential brain power that we use is probably nearer 4% than 10%.

Most of us, then, appear to let 96% of our mental potential lie unused. But it doesn't have to be so. Once we begin to understand how the brain's memory works, the way is opened to tap that vast unused potential. The result can be a quantum leap in learning speed, an enrichment of every part of our life and, scientists now believe, a measurable increase in intelligence, whatever our age.

First, let us look at some of the facts

Neurons

The average adult human brain consists of some 12,000 to 15,000 million nerve cells. (15,000,000,000). That is about three times the entire population of the earth.

The human nervous system, controlled by the brain, begins its development only 20 days after conception. Five weeks from conception brain development starts in earnest and after eight weeks the first of two brain spurts begins. At this stage the brain represents half the total length of the foetus (although it is still only ½ inch long!). This is when the neuroblasts begin to grow. Neuroblasts are embryonic cells that will in turn become neurons, or brain nerve cells. The speed at which neuroblasts are now developing is staggering. They are added at the rate of several thousand a *minute*.

Nutrition is vital during the formation of brain cells. Of particular importance is adequate protein to provide adequate amounts of amino acids. Tryptophan is especially important for brain biochemistry and human milk has twice as much of this amino acid as cows milk. In societies where mothers are undernourished, children may have up to 50% less neurons than their counterparts among Western children. Additionally, the part of the brain responsible for limb co-ordination can be seriously impaired.

Twelve weeks after conception, the tiny foetus is now adding neurons at the rate of 2,000 a *second.* To put this into context, an adult honey bee's brain contains some 7,000 neurons. A bee can accomplish many sophisticated tasks, including building and maintaining a honeycomb, calculating distance, signalling to its companions the direction of pollen sources, and recognizing a course by sight and smell. All with the number of neurons the human foetus develops in under 3 seconds. About twenty weeks after conception or 18 weeks *before* birth, the human embryo has laid down its entire nervous system: 12-15 billion neurons. Whilst the number of neurons is important, of even greater significance is the next stage of brain development: the second brain spurt.

About ten weeks before birth, each neuron starts to send out numerous thin fibres to make actual and potential connections with other neurons. The power of the brain is largely a function of the *number* of neurons and the *richness* of their connections. Since each neuron can itself make thousands of connections, the potential number of inter-connections in the brain runs into trillions. The key point to remember is that only some of these connections are made automatically. Most are made by using the brain. The more your brain is stimulated, the richer the connections and the higher your practical mental ability. Many of the basic interconnections are made before the age of five!

The human head will grow in physical size four-fold after birth. The evolutionary limit to the size of the baby's head at birth has been set by the size of the mother's birth canal. By age five, the skull will be 90% of adult size. Full adult size is, in fact, reached at about age ten. The brain now weighs about 3lbs. That is about 2% of the body, yet the brain requires 20% of the oxygen supply.

Oxygen is so vital to the brain that, should the human be restricted in oxygen intake, the supply will be automatically reduced to all other parts of the body before supplies to the brain are diminished. Not surprisingly, oxygen is equally vital before birth. The foetus of a woman who smokes receives less oxygen, and the subsequent reading scores of such children are generally below those of non-smoking mothers.

The role of nutrition in brain development is as important in the early years after birth as it is before birth, since malnutrition will not only reduce the number of neurons, but also the number of connections between nerve cells. In studies on rats, it has been found that neuron connection can be reduced by 40% simply due to poor nutrition. The reason, in passing, why the long-suffering rat is so frequently studied is that its nervous system is quite similar to that of the human. Some readers will no doubt draw other behavioral parallels.

We have seen how the number of neurons in the brain is fixed before birth. Unlike any other body cells, brain cells do not usually regenerate themselves. However, even if they did die, at the rate of several thousand a day, the loss over a lifetime would be trivial and quite unlikely to affect practical mental ability.

Of far greater significance is the fact that the number of connections between neurons is continuously growing, and this would more than compensate. In fact it would argue for an improvement of mental ability with age - and as we shall see, if an improvement is the expectation, that is indeed the result.

So far we have been speaking of "the neuron". This gives a misleading picture of simplicity. In fact the neuron consists of a cell body (the grey matter) from which leads a principal fibre called the axon. The axon is covered by a fatty coating called myelin and it may terminate either in a connection with another neuron cell, or with branch-like fibres called dendrites. The axon and dendrites are the white matter of the brain.

To over-simplify, the axon transmits the electrical impulses that mark the working of the brain, the dendrites receive them. Gluing the whole brain together, and nourishing it, are glia cells (from the greek glia meaning 'glue'). If you were somewhat surprised by the numbers involved in 15 billion brain cells, and were astonished that there are hundreds of times more dendrites, you may choose not even to try to comprehend the fact that there are probably 100 billion glia cells in the human brain. The mind really does boggle at its own complexity!

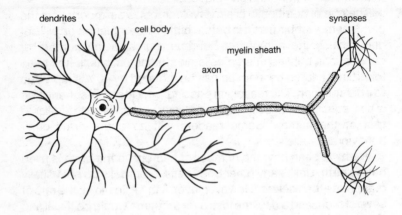

The junction at which two nerve cells meet, or at which dendrite meets dendrite, is called the synapse. This is a tiny gap, and the electrical activity of the brain is conducted down the axon to the synapse. A connection is made when one of a number of chemicals is released to bridge the gap at the synapse. These chemicals are called neuro-transmitters and they permit electrical activity to flow across the synapse. The speed of transmission of a neurological impulse is about 100 metres a second. The *transmission* of brain activity then is not electrical, but a physical/chemical reaction to an original electrical impulse.

We now know that there are up to 30 different types of neuro-transmitter. Some are amines, most are amino acids, the building blocks of protein.

We also know that neuro-transmitters not only transmit an impulse but are capable of modifying it along the way - although we do not yet know how. When we do, we may begin to unlock the physical secrets of memory and thought. That is a breakthrough comparable to the initial cracking of the 'double helix' genetic code, by Crick and Watson.

Sexual differences in Brain Development

Whilst physical development of the brain is largely complete by age five, there are further well established intervals of intellectual development at ages 6 to 8, 10 to 12 and 14 to 16. It seems that we should try to ensure that educational stimuli should be timed to coincide with these natural periods of development.

It is worth noting that psychological researcher H.T. Epstein, has pointed out that the brain development of girls at age 11 is up to twice that of boys, whilst something like the converse is true at age 15.

This could argue for a different curriculum for girls at these ages, with a much more complex and challenging input at 11 and less intensity at 15.

Why so big?

"The creative capacity of the human brain may be, for all practical purposes infinite."
Educational Technology
"We are only now on the threshold of knowing the range of the educability of man - the perfectability of man. We have never addressed ourselves to this problem before."
Dr. Jerome Bruner, Harvard University
"We will by conscious command, evolve cerebral centres which will permit us to use powers that we now are not even capable of imagining."
Dr. Frederic Tilney. Leading French Brain Specialist.
"We are hoarding potentials so great that they are just about unimaginable."
Jack Schwartz, Psycho-physical trainer.

Just what is the potential that causes sober scientists to indulge in such spine tingling prophecies?

The fundamental determinant of the brain's potential is the number of connections it can make. With 10-15 billion nerve cells, each one capable of making thousands of contacts, the possible permutations of connections runs into the trillions.

Yet this massive brain potential was acquired not by astronaut man, but by Neanderthal man, because the 3lb human brain has not physically changed much in the last 50,000 years. Our hunter gatherer ancestors had similar sized brains to ours, but they clearly were not so intelligent, in the sense of the measurable and practical application of intelligence.

There have been five pre-historic landmarks in the use, rather than mere possession, of this vast potential intelligence: walking on two legs, increasing manual dexterity, tool-making, speech and writing.

"Speech alone has rendered man Human" wrote the eighteenth century theologian Herder. Speech enabled us to pass on advice so that each generation did not have to learn everything from scratch. We know from the study of primitive societies that a four-hundred word vocabulary will facilitate most basic communication, and an adult today can survive very well on 4,000 basic words of his own language.

The next landmark was the invention of printing, which enabled experience and concepts to be passed on to all who could read. You will learn in later chapters that educators believe mental ability can demonstratively be increased if a child learns to read early and to read widely. *The brain is the only organ that expands through use.* The more it is used, either to acquire facts or in the process of creativity, the more memory associations are formed. The more associations are formed, the easier it is to remember previously acquired information, *and* also to form new associations, i.e. create new ideas and concepts. This is a vitally important "virtuous circle", and reading is a key to forming it.

But this brief history only helps to explain how man has, quite slowly, come to make an increasing practical use of a fraction of his mental capabilities. it does not explain *why* we have such a large brain., Evolution is rarely so profligate. As Arthur Koestler put it -

"It is the only example of evolution providing a species with an organ which it does not know how to use, a luxury organ, which will take its owner thousands of years to learn to put to proper use - if it ever does."

Of course, our brain was our competitive advantage in achieving the dominant position in the animal kingdom. But it did not need to be anywhere as advanced. Man in the last 50 years has attained near-magical achievements in the technical sphere. He is gaining control over his physical environment at an exponential rate of progress.

However, progress in finding solutions to more philosophical questions has been either non-existent or painfully slow. We appear to have more than adequate brain power to solve material problems. What we need is a parallel improvement in our ability to develop new conceptual solutions, to such age old problems as injustice, and international combativeness.

It is no accident that our material success is largely due to the fact that we are trained to think in a pattern we call logical, and as we shall shortly see, this seems to mainly involve one side of the brain - the left side. Conversely our learning methods are generally not designed to stimulate the development of the side of the brain that processes concepts - the right side. So our success in logical, material pursuits is perhaps not surprising - nor is our comparative failure in conceptual ethical issues.

Left Brain/Right Brain

That the brain is divided physically into a left and right half is not a new discovery. The Egyptians knew that the left side of the brain controlled and received sensations from the right side of the body and vice versa.

It is only in the last two dozen years, however, that the true implication of the left/right split has gradually become apparent, through the work of a number of researchers. The most famous are probably Dr. Roger Sperry and Dr. Robert Ornstein of the California Institute of Technology. Their work has won them a Nobel prize.

Sperry and Ornstein noted that the left and the right hemispheres are connected by an incredibly complex network of up to 300 million nerve fibres called the Corpus Callosum. They were also able to show that the two halves of the brain tend to have different functions.

They and other researchers indicate that the left brain primarily appears to deal with language and mathematical processes and logical thought, sequences, analysis and what we generally label academic pursuits.

The right brain principally deals with music, and visual impressions, pictures, spatial patterns, and colour recognition. They also ascribe to the right brain the ability to deal with certain kinds of conceptual thought - intangible 'ideas' such as love, loyalty, beauty.

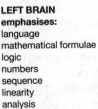

LEFT BRAIN emphasises:
language
mathematical formulae
logic
numbers
sequence
linearity
analysis
words of a song

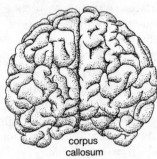

corpus
callosum

RIGHT BRAIN emphasises:
forms and patterns
spatial manipulation
rhythm and
musical appreciation
images/pictures
imagination
daydreaming
dimension
tune of a song

Back view of the two sides of your brain and their probable functions

The specialisation of the two halves of the brain can result in some bizarre behaviour. Patients who, for medical reasons, have had their corpus callosum severed, have effectively two semi-independent brains: two minds in one head.

If a ball is shown to the left visual field of such a person, i.e. registered to their *right* brain hemisphere, the speaking half of the brain, which is in the other, (left) brain will claim to have seen nothing. If, however, the patient is asked to feel in a bag of assorted shapes he will correctly pull out a ball. If he is asked what he has done he will say 'nothing'. The ball has only been seen with the right brain, and felt with the right brain. The speech centre, which is located in the left brain, has registered nothing.

Even more delicate experiments have been performed on surgically split-brained patients. The word **SINBAD** was projected to such a patient while his eyes were focused on the precise spot between N and B. The first 3 letters went to his right brain, the last three to his left hemisphere. When asked to *say* what he had seen, he replied **BAD.** When asked to *point* with his left hand to what he had seen he pointed to the word **SIN**.

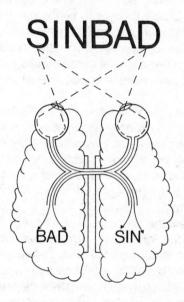

The specialisation of the two brains has also been demonstrated by measuring the electrical activity of the brain during various activities.

When the brain is relaxed in a state of rest, it tends predominantly to show an alpha brain wave rhythm - i.e. waves of 8/10 cycles per second. Ornstein found that a subject tackling a mathematical problem showed an increase in alpha in the right hemisphere. This indicated that the right side was relaxing whilst the left was active and, therefore, in a beta brain wave pattern. In contrast, when a subject was matching coloured patterns, the left showed alpha (i.e. was resting) and the right showed beta (i.e. was active).

The brain scans reproduced in Chapter 7, show the varying levels of electrical brain activity in a subject listening to music, words and singing.

The first activity (music) involved the right brain.

The second (listening to words only) involved the left brain, but singing (words and music together) involved the whole brain.

The left brain is now thought to be the half that specialises in serial, sequential thought, i.e. analysing information in sequence in a "logical" step by step approach. The left *rationalises.*

The right brain seems to take in several bits of information "at a glance" and process them into one overall thought. The right *synthesises.*

When you meet someone it seems to be the right brain that takes all the elements at once and synthesises the pattern into a whole to recognise the person instantaneously. If you were using your left brain only you would probably scan first the hair, then the forehead, then the eyes, nose, mouth and chin in sequence to "build up" a picture. The right brain, however, recognises the pattern immediately.

It is the left brain that is dominant in, for example, mathematical calculations. It is the right brain that processes non-verbal signals.

We have come as a society to stress, and value more highly, the functions of the left brain. The analytical thinking of the physicist is usually valued higher (in money terms) than the artistic and intuitive ability of the musician or artist. Most schools relegate right brain dominant activities to two or three periods a week. Yet those schools who have tried increasing the proportion of arts subjects, have found that levels of *all* scholastic performance improved. Because, although the two halves of the brain may indeed be specialised, they are far from being isolated. Each compliments and improves the performance of the other.

Education that emphasises only analytical thinking is literally "single minded". As one psychologist put it *"Such people's brains are being systematically damaged. In many ways they are being de-educated."*

Two Brains are Better than One!

It would appear that the better connected the two halves of the brain, the greater the potential of the brain for learning and creativity.

Recent research by Dr. Christine de Lacoste Utamsing at the University of Texas has found that the interconnecting area is always larger and probably richer in nerve fibres in women than in men. We don't know why yet, but it has fascinating implications.

Roger Sperry's work further showed that, when people develop a particular mental skill, it produced a positive improvement in all areas of mental activity, including those that are lying dormant. In other words, the popular belief that painters and musicians (right brain people) must inevitably be poor at mathematics is not true.

Einstein, who actually failed mathematics at school, was a creditable violinist and artist, and has described the insight that gave birth to his Theory of Relativity. Alone on a hill on a summer day, he was daydreaming, and imagined himself riding a sunbeam to the far edge of the universe; but in his mind's eye he saw himself returning towards the sun. That flash of inspiration, (which as we shall see was probably associated with a theta brain-wave pattern), suggested that for the dream to come true, it required the universe to be curved. Space, light and time had to be curved also.

The Theory of Relativity is therefore a good example of left brain/right brain synchronised thought.

Since the state of reverie or daydreaming is associated with a predominantly theta and alpha wave pattern, it is also a perfect example of how an alpha brain-wave state creates the meditative background conditions for creativity.

Leonardo da Vinci is often quoted as probably the best example in history of the genius that can be liberated when left and right brain activities are fully combined. He was the most accomplished artist, mathematician and scientist of his day in at least half a dozen different fields, and he could write simultaneously with his left and right hand. The artist Sir Edwin Landseer, had a similar ability he used as a popular party trick. He could draw a horse with one hand, whilst simultaneously drawing a deer with the other!

Now this is not to say that there is a rigorous demarcation between the left and right hemispheres of the brain. Each half contributes to the majority of thoughts, but there is no doubt about a specialisation of the two brains. There are cases where patients had lost the power of speech (left brain) but could still sing (right brain).

In the animal kingdom, the bottlenose dolphin is a mammal that has exceptional mental powers and has, according to the Severstsov Institute in Moscow evolved an extraordinary brain. It can sleep with one half or hemisphere of its brain whilst maintaining full consciousness in the other half. Then after an hour or so it switches brains! Moreover, during sleep one eye remains open and the other remains shut.

The dolphin is also capable of incredible feats of memory. Lyall Watson has described how a dolphin can emit a half hour "song" - a series of high pitched sounds that appear to be the main form of dolphin communication. The dolphin can then repeat the exact same sequence of sounds in an identical half hour repeat performance. It's rather like repeating a half hour soliloquy verbatim.

Educational researchers are talking increasingly of 'whole brain learning'. Joseph Bogen, writing in the U.C.L.A. Educator , remarks *"The current emphasis in education on the acquisition of verbal skills and the development of analytical thought processes, neglects the development of non-verbal abilities."* It is, he claims *"starving one half of the brain and ignoring its contribution to the whole person."*

Since non-verbal communication is a right brain activity and non-verbal actions account for perhaps 80% of all communication, we can see just how much our left brain orientated learning systems may be starving our intellectual development.

Stuart Dimond, a former Professor of Psychology at Cardiff, points out in his book 'The Double Brain', *"when the two hemispheres work together they perform much better than one."*

Dr. Bernard Glueck at the Institute for Living in Hartford, Connecticut found that men and women practising meditation showed an increased synchronicity between the left and right sides of the brain, and suggested that this showed an improved communication through the corpus callosum, achieved by the attainment of relaxation and increased alpha brain waves.

Surveys of creative thinking have emphasised the importance of encouraging an initial right brain visualisation, an intuitive solution, which can subsequently be evaluated logically by left brain processes. But the original impetus is from the non-verbal side of our brain.

Left v Right in our culture

The distinction between left and right is deep in the human pysche, and is constant amongst all cultures. It has much significance.

Right is a synonym for correct. Righteousness is good. The angels sit on God's right hand. Right in Latin is "dexter", from which we get dexterity.

Left in Latin is "sinistra" from which we get sinister. In French left is "gauche".

About ninety per cent of humans are right handed, and more girls than boys. Newborn babies will turn four times more frequently to the right than the left, but left-handedness is more common in twins. The speech centres in the brain (Broca's area and Wernicke's area) are located in the left brain, which controls the right side of the body.

It is important to be 'right-eared', because a high proportion of dyslexics 'lead' naturally with their left ear. Sound entering through the right ear travels the shortest neurological path across the brain to the left hemisphere, whereas sound entering the left ear follows a longer neurological path to reach the right brain.

It is logical to ask whether left handed people - the 10% minority - also have the left brain as the dominant hemisphere for speech. Or do they, process speech with their right brains? Generally, they do not; but an important 35% of left handers do activate their right brain (as well as left brain) while speaking, In contrast only 10% of natural right handers do so.

The Triune Brain

The brain is not only divided horizontally into left and right. It is effectively divided vertically as well. Dr Paul Maclean in 1973 coined the term triune brain to emphasise the three divisions.

(1) The Reptilian brain (or brainstem), which emerges directly from the spinal column and controls the very basic instinctive responses.

(2) The Limbic system or mammalian brain, which includes amongst other organs, the hypothalamus and the pituitary gland. It is this mini brain that controls emotions, sexuality and the pleasure centres.

(3) Finally the Neo-Cortex, which controls the intellectual processes which we have been discussing.

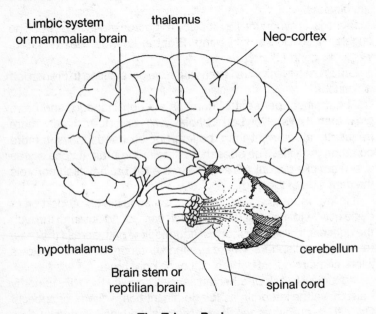

The Triune Brain

The three parts of the brain show the evolution of the brain from pure instinctual responses, via the acquisition of controlled emotional response and the beginning of memory, to the incredible complexity of the new brain or neo-cortex.

It is of great significance that the limbic system tends to be the conduit through which impulses are transferred from instinctual, involuntary behaviour to 'rational' thought. Your personality is determined by the interaction of the limbic system and your neo-cortex. Psychologists now believe that most learning also involves an interaction between your old and new brains via the limbic system.

Many other scientists in the last few years have increasingly come to the conclusion that the key to more effective learning may lie in the limbic system, since it controls the emotions, and an appeal to the emotions is by far the most effective way to create attention and memory.

In 1971 Rappaport* concluded that emotion is not only involved in memory but is actually the basis on which memory is organised. Recently Luiz Machado, Head of the University of Rio de Janeiro, a prime mover in the Accelerated Learning Movement, claimed that if new material was presented in such a way as to produce emotional arousal, i.e. involve the limbic system, it would activate mental powers not normally used.

Since the limbic system exerts a powerful effect at the subconscious level, he may well be correct. Certainly the activation of the full power of the brain through the subconscious is a theme that we shall return to again and again throughout this book.

Does Mental Ability decline with Age?

Almost certainly not. What *does* deteriorate is the body. Arteries become clogged as fat builds up inside the walls, and once they have passed fifty years of age, up to 50% of people suffer diminution of blood supply, i.e. oxygen feeding the brain. When these arteries are cleaned, patients show a significant reduction in nervousness, mental distress and a measurable increase in I.Q. Moreover, when older patients are given specific oxygen treatment, there can often be an appreciable improvement in mental ability.

It has also been found that a high blood pressure correlates with loss of mental ability, and when hypertension and blood pressure

* "Emotions and Memory" D.A. Rappaport. International Universities Press.

is reduced, by relaxation exercises or dieting for example, brain function improves.

Mental activity involves complicated physio-chemical activity. In fact Dr. David Samuels of the Weizman Institute estimates that there may well be up to a million chemical reactions taking place in the brain in any one minute! Yet there is no evidence that these chemical reactions become any less frequent with age; indeed the production of R.N.A., a key and complex chemical involved in memory, actually increases as you get older.

The impression that older people's memory for more recent events is poorer than for further events is perhaps because there are normally fewer outstanding events to remember as one grows older. The novel experiences are mostly encountered in younger years. And novelty aids memory.

Use it - or lose it

Whilst there is no major reason - and certainly no need - for there to be a reduction in mental powers with ageing, there certainly is conclusive evidence that the provision of constant stimuli improves mental ability.

Mark Rosenweig at U.C.L.A. conducted an experiment on three groups of rats.

Group 1 lived in a cage full of wheels, ladders, toys, mazes, etc.

Group 2 lived in an impoverished environment without any stimulation.

Group 3 could see the richer environment in an adjoining cage but could not join in.

Later examination of the three groups showed that group 1 rats, who had directly interacted with a challenging environment, all had a heavier and thicker cerebral cortex, whereas neither the observer rats nor the environmentally deprived rats had any increase in brain size.

The conclusion is that it is necessary to be *involved* in mental exercise, to experiment directly with new ideas. Many acknowledged intellectuals who have lived to a ripe old age bear out this truth. Tennyson, Wordsworth, Bernard Shaw, Einstein, Bertrand Russell, Haydn, Bach, Rembrandt, Michelangelo, were all doing work of extraordinary quality in the latter part of their lives.

We have already seen how adequate oxygen intake is important and regular breaks from mental work and taking exercise is important. The Greeks instinctively realised this. Their senators would regularly pace up and down their forum during debates.

Nature or Nurture?

The way in which the brain actually develops enables us to dispose of the question of whether intelligence is a function of heredity (nature) or environment (nurture). The answer is "Both". The number of brain cells is a factor; but the way those brain cells are stimulated to make rich connections is far more significant.

Thus it is probably correct to say that almost every normal child is born a potential genius.

Even if innate intelligence is merely average, a rich intellectual environment during the period of the second brain growth spurt, with plenty of opportunities to learn, can ensure the development of a greater proportion of the brain potential than would normally be expected.

The anecdotal evidence for this in humans (as well as clinical evidence in rats!) is overwhelming.

Genius is more made than born

In 1800 Karl Witte's father, a German doctor, decided to give his son a really rich educational environment. Karl entered the University of Leipzig at nine, and gained his PhD at fourteen!

Lord Kelvin's mother made the same decision. Her son became one of the nineteenth century's most successful physicists.

More recently in the well publicised "Edith Experiment", New Yorker Aaron Stern determined, in 1952, to give his daughter the best environment he could devise. Classical music was a continuous background. He talked to her in adult terms and showed her reading cards with numbers and animals on them.

Edith Stern could talk in simple sentences at one, and had read an entire volume of the Encyclopedia Brittannica by the age of five. She was reading six books a day by age six. At twelve she enrolled in college and was teaching higher mathematics at Michigan State University at fifteen years old. She scores 200 on a scale where 155 is genius.

In England, Ruth Lawrence who passed her 'O' level maths at nine and 'A' level at ten (normally 18) was accepted at Oxford University at twelve years of age., She had been educated in an intellectually rich environment by her parents.

We shall be returning in a later chapter to the subject of pre-school learning. We shall also be debating the perfectly reasonable concern that **no** child should be 'forced' like an intellectual hot-house plant. Clearly, it is vital that the child should become a socially well integrated adult, enjoy her childhood and *never* be pressured. The point to make here, however, is that there is no question that a loving, relaxed and *rich* environment during the vital formative years definitely does create a higher degree of mental capability. And that is of undeniable benefit.

This benefit is not merely related to intellectual performance. The largest long term study of outstanding ability was started in California by Dr. Terman. Commencing in 1925, it has followed the progress of 1000 gifted children (all above 135 I.Q.s). It has concluded, so far, that:

* Physical health and growth was above normal.
* Marriage rates were average/divorce rates were below average.
* 70% graduated (7½ *times* normal)

Society has come to be somewhat perversely suspicious of genius. Almost as if there is something rather 'unfair' about actively encouraging mental growth.

As researchers of this book, we have come to believe in all-round education. We are totally against parents indulging their own ego's by pressurising their children to succeed. But we are equally unhappy about the attitude of mind that prompted a Manchester mother, when she was told that her son had an I.Q. of 167, to say . . . *"But he's such a nice boy."*

The truth is we can indeed improve our children's ability and our own. And that is surely a challenge we must accept.

Alpha, Beta, Theta, Delta

The brain generates tiny electrical pulses as thoughts traverse the labyrinth of the mind. The physical conduits of these thoughts are the millions of nerve cells or neurons in the brain. Just as radio signals, in order to make a comprehensible message, are beamed out on radio waves, a band of signals within a defined frequency, so the brain's activity also occurs in waves. Brain waves can be measured on an electro-encephalograph machine (which is normally abbreviated to E.E.G. Machine). By attaching sensitive electrodes to the scalp, it is possible to measure accurately the type of brain wave that a subject is producing. These waves are usually expressed in the number of cycles per second (or C.P.S.)

The brain produces 4 main frequencies:

Beta level brain waves - range 13-25 C.P.S. (cycles per second)

Alpha level brain waves - range 8-12 C.P.S.

Theta level brain waves - range 4-7 C.P.S.

Delta level brain waves - range 0.5-3 C.P.S.

The following chart relates each type of brain wave to its principal function. We must remember however, that when we speak of someone being 'in alpha' we mean that this is their characteristic and predominant brain wave. Other brain waves will also be present, but in smaller quantities than usual.

Brain Wave   Normal Activity

BETA β

13-25 CPS

This is the brain wave of your 'conscious' mind, it characterises logical thought, analysis and action. You are wide awake and alert, figuring out complex problems, talking, speaking, doing.

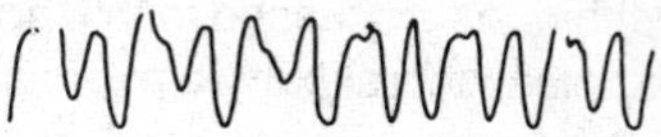

ALPHA α

8-12 CPS

This is the brain wave that characterises relaxation and meditation, The state of mind during which you daydream, let your imagination run. It is a state of relaxed alertness that facilitates inspiration, fast assimilation of facts, and heightened memory. Alpha lets your reach your subconscious, and since your self image is primarily in your subconscious, it is the only effective way to reach it.

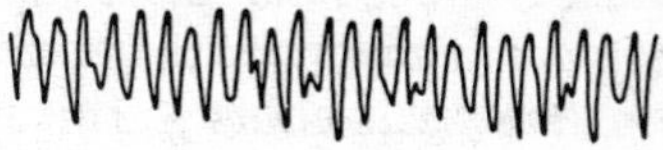

23

THETA θ
4-7 CPS

Deep meditation and reverie. The twilight zone associated with creativity, high suggestibility and flashes of inspiration. Dominant during ages 2 - 5.

DELTA δ
0.5-3 CPS

Deep dreamless sleep

The linking of left and right brain activities is important in producing a shift from learning to accelerated learning. Yet our society is very 'beta orientated'. We are busy thinking about the problem in hand, but don't leave ourselves sufficiently open to other influences, which would help us memorize faster and make the sort of less expected connections that we call creative thinking.

In beta you don't see the wood for concentrating on the trees. But learn to relax, increase the proportion of the alpha and ideally theta brain waves, and you have created the conditions where you may begin to see the whole picture. 'Alpha' is a natural and receptive state of mind, that we can all attain through the techniques discussed in this book. They principally involve simple and pleasant relaxation exercises and listening to certain types of music.

The theta brain wave pattern is especially interesting. It occurs spontaneously to most of us in the twilight state between being fully awake and falling asleep. Arthur Koestler called it 'reverie'. This drowsy stage is associated with fleeting semi-hallucinatory images. Thousands of artistic and literary inspirations and scientific inventions have been credited to this state, a sort of free-form thinking that puts you in touch with your subconscious.

Many psychologists would agree it is a reasonable hypothesis that, when left/right brain symbiosis takes place, conscious and subconscious are also united. The proportion of theta brain waves becomes much higher than normal. This is the moment when logical left brain activity declines. The left brain, which normally acts as a filter or censor to the subconscious, drops its guard, and allows the more intuitive, emotional and creative depths of the right brain to become increasingly influential.

If the hypothesis is true, then do women, popularly characterised as more intuitive, reach a walking theta state more often than men; and can this be associated with the fact that their left/right brain link, the corpus callosum, is larger and richer in connective capabilities than men's? We do not yet know, but it is a fascinating area for future research.

At the University of Colorado Medical Centre and at the Biofeedback Centre in Denver, Dr. Thomas Budzyski has found that, when people were trained to achieve and maintain theta brain waves using biofeedback techniques, they did indeed learn much faster. Moreover, many emotional and attitudinal problems were solved at the same time.

For example, in a theta state, suggestions that racial prejudice is wrong were well accepted. Suggestions to overweight people to follow a sensible eating pattern were accepted and subsequently complied with, and insomnia and drinking problems were successfuly tackled.

Some time ago a New York advertising agency was asked to produce a T.V. Commercial to combat racial prejudice. They produced two. The first used a carefully built up rational argument. The second was a highly emotional film featuring attractive young black children and using many subconscious but positive appeals for fairness.

The logical T.V. Commercial actually intensified the degree of racial prejudice. The subjects felt themselves threatened as they realized they could not give an equally dispassionate and rational counter argument. Consequently the only possible response was an aggressive defence involving an increased emotional commitment to their original attitude.

The second commercial however, worked. Emotion laden appeals went beyond the conscious, the intellectual objections, and created a new positive image at the subconscious level that changed the subject's entire personal response, so no conflict or threat was aroused.

Can intelligence be increased?

Whilst it is certainly an oversimplification to relate intelligence to brain capacity it is, however, interesting to relate three statements:

The average I.Q. is 100

The genius-level is 160

The average human probably uses 4% of his potential brain power

If that average human could learn to use not 4% of his brain but a still minimal 7% of his brain, could he attain genius level?

This book is about techniques that probably improve the human memory, that increase creativity and that provide access to unused brain power. The indications are that the same techniques can measurably improve intelligence.

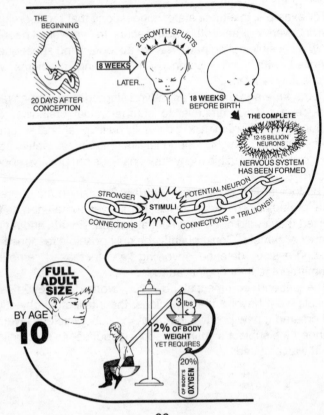

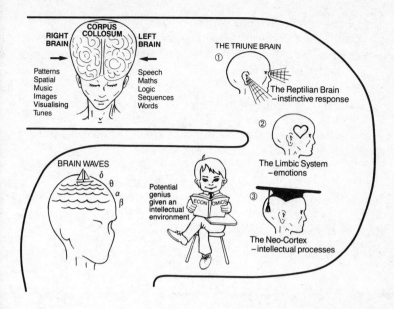

The above "Memory Map" is our way of visualising the main points in the chapter in an easy to remember form.

THE BASIS OF MEMORY

There is no learning without memory. From the primitive creature, who merely learns instinctive reflex behaviour through repeated exposure to a particular set of circumstances, to the Polish memorists who have memorised word for word all 12 volumes of the Talmud, learning involves memory.

Yet surprisingly there is not yet an agreement as to how memory really works.

This book is about the evolution of an advanced and accelerated learning method, not a detailed text book on psychology. Nevertheless it is important that you are familiar with the latest conclusions on memory from clinical psychology.

More than one Memory

Most psychologists now agree that there are at least two memories: short term memory and long term memory. The short term memory, as Dr. Alan Baddeley describes it, seems to be the working memory.

If you want to multiply 28 x 3 in your head, you would use the short term memory to do the calculation, and then, if it were significant enough, commit the answer to your long term memory. The short-term memory is, effectively, a temporary storage device.

When you are reading a sentence, it is your short term memory that retains the words at the beginning of the sentence for long enough to make sense of the whole sentence. Then it is the *meaning,* rather than the individual words, that is transferred into your long term memory. The long term memory is the permanent storage system from which recall can be made.

The short term memory seems to analyse, the long term memory seems to synthesise.

Interestingly, the design work that has gone into producing computers has recognised this distinction.

A computer is divided into a working memory - the Random Access Memory (RAM), which is the processing and calculating part, and a storage memory called the Read Only Memory (ROM).

If you switch off the computer the RAM contents disappear, just as those of the short term memory seem to. They must be recorded onto a disc or tape (or incorporated into the form of a permanent ROM chip) if they are to be stored permanently.

How Short is Short?

There have been some interesting experiments designed to estimate the time span of the short term memory. If you take a glowing stick from a bonfire and rotate it fast enough in the dark, it will appear to produce a full circle of light. This is because the sensory memory - a specialist part of your short term memory - retains the image of the light long enough for the actual light to return back to its starting point on the circle.

In the same way, a cinema film is a series of still pictures with very short periods of darkness in between. In order to see the film as continuous action, you need to hold the image of the last frame in your short term memory until the appearance of the next frame, and relate them together in such a way as to produce an impression of continuous movement.

The time span of this type of sensory short term memory is probably about 1/10 of a second.

The time span of the short term memory acting as a working memory - to calculate or to read - is a matter of some discussion. Baddeley conducted experiments on the way words were memorised. He found that a series of long words was less well recalled than a series of short words, probably because the subjects, in order to remember the list, were *sub-vocalising* the words, i.e. hearing the words in their 'mind's ear'.

Clearly the longer the words, the longer it took to sub-vocalise them, and the subjects could only remember as much as they could say in 15 seconds. As would be predicted by the theory, fast talkers could remember more!

Researchers Waugh and Norman, writing in 'The Psychological Review' in 1965, confirmed that the number of unrelated numbers a person can recall after just one presentation rarely exceeds 10 - about the same number that could be spoken or heard in your mind's ear in 15 seconds.

They also identified an auditory and visual short term memory, and commented that reading aloud was helpful since it helped to register (encode) the material in the short term auditory store as well as the short term visual store.

This point is important, because other researchers have found that the process of rehearsal involved in the sub-vocalisation, is critical to transferring information from the short to the long term memory. Unless an item is rehearsed, it is lost out of the short term memory, and does not enter the long term memory.

Other researchers also calculate a short term memory of about 15 seconds in span. Carroll (1966) deduces this from the work of simultaneous translators, who have to hold a sentence or sentences in their short term memory and translate with only the briefest of delays. The same indication (of a 15 second span) is implicit in the ability of court reporters to hold 10-15 second's worth of evidence before transcription.

Electrical v Chemical

No-one knows exactly how memory is created in the physical sense. But a recent series of experiments indicate that short term memory involves a primarily electrical activity in the brain, and long term memory involves a predominantly chemical process, and the possible modification of proteins.

Researchers Flood and Jarvik have reported that drugs which affect the synthesis of proteins, or their transfer along the axons, only affect long term memory, whereas drugs, that affect electrical activity in the brain appear only to affect short term memory.

Other experiments support the view that long term memory involves chemical changes. Thus researcher J.V. McConnell began research in 1966 which showed that RNA (ribonucleic acid) was involved in learning, and that learned behaviour could be transferred from one rat to another by exchanging RNA from one brain to another.

In 1970 George Ungar at the Bayer College of Medicine, Houston, Texas taught a group of rats to be afraid of the dark. He then isolated a particular protein from the brains of those rats and injected it into the brains of untrained rats - who immediately showed the same fear of the dark! Subsequently he reproduced

31

the protein artificially, (he named it Scotophobin, from the Greek for fear of the dark), and found that the artificial protein, when injected into normal rats, had the same effect. They too became frightened of the dark.

Since then, other researchers have found that Scotophobin when injected into goldfish teaches them to fear the dark; so the specific amino acid chain in this particular protein may have a universal significance.

Yet further teams of researchers have identified brain chemicals that discriminate between colours.

Scientists are already working on direct computer brain symbiosis (the direct linking of a human mind to a computer). It seems that we now have two futuristic avenues for research: artificial learning by electrical input (computer/brain links) and artificial learning by chemical input.

There seem to be parts of the day when learning is optimum usually later rather than earlier. This may also be due to the fact the body goes through a complex hormonal and chemical cycle throughout the day, and this cycle may well be influential on the production of the chemicals which result in the consolidation of memory traces.

When we talk of memory in future pages we shall mean long term memory.

Memory as a Three Way Activity

We talk loosely about memory, but there are actually three distinct aspects to memorising something. The three 'R's' of memory, are Registration, Retention and Recall.

You have to:-

(1) Become aware of new facts and make an *active* effort to transfer them to long term memory. That is Registration or as psychologists term it 'encoding'.
(2) Store these facts in your long term memory and
(3) Be able to recall the facts when you need them.

Psychologists often refer to the "tip-of-the-tongue phenomenon" to illustrate the difference between recognition and recall. This is the common experience of feeling you know a name, for example, and perhaps even the initial letter of that name, yet are unable to recall it accurately and completely.

Clearly the memory is there, because you almost always recognise the name when it is eventually given - but cannot recall it fully without aid.

When faced with an apparently new learning task, it is sometimes difficult to comprehend just how fast our recall can be. If you are a fast talker, for example, you may speak at about 170-190 words a minute and the words will be produced in correct grammatical order. It seems like a reflex action, but the mechanism clearly involves an astonishing display of logic manipulation (in the short term memory) and retrieval of the correct grammar and vocabulary (from the long term memory), coupled with a possible simultaneous use of right brain to conceptualise and left brain to speak forth the conclusions. Not for the first (or last) time in this book the mind may well marvel at its own complexity!

That the three activities of Registration, Retention and Recall are not necessarily the same is easily proved. Consider the following list of words and repeat them twice. (That's the encoding part).

Test No 1

Fox	Play
Place	Spy
Pen	Lamp
Tree	Full
Book	Sink
Far	Water
Easy	Grass
Bike	Sand

Now look away and write down as many words as possible. Then look back at the list. Do you 'recognise' all the words? If you do, then clearly you remember them, in the sense that you acknowledge you have seen them before. So the memory was there, but it is unlikely that you will actually have recalled them all correctly. Potential memory is invariably greater than actual recall. Recall is not the same as recognition. It is incidentally, clear in testing old people that if their memory deteriorates at all, it is the ability to recall that declines, not the ability to create or store information.

The distinction between memory defined as *recognition* of facts or events when we are reminded or "given a clue" and memory defined as the ability to *recall* without a prompt is an important one. It is the reason why the accurate measurement of learning is quite difficult and why it is important to agree a definition of learning before hand.

Here is a suggestion. As you read through this book, note down any fact or conclusion, that you think would be important in creating the ideal learning programme.

You might, for example, have concluded that, without rehearsal of a new fact in the short term memory, it would not get transferred to the long term memory. You might also have concluded from Chapter One that, since your brain's potential capacity is so obviously enormous, the requirement of any learning system, is not that it should increase your intelligence but that it should release a fraction of the talent you already have.

If you actively make notes, you will not only obtain much more benefit from this book - you will learn something fundamental about memory and about learning itself.

The Model of Memory

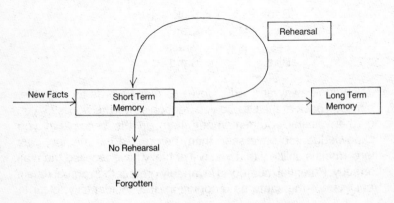

34

Numerous researchers have conducted experiments which indicate that information which is not rehearsed in the short term memory is rapidly forgotten. Conversely, there seems to be a direct correlation between the amount of rehearsal and the probability that the material will be recalled. Murdoch and Waugh (1963) showed that the probability of recalling a word that had been listened to for 2 seconds was almost twice the probability of recalling a word that had been listened to for 1 second.

This is because the short term memory is the part of the memory that does the encoding, or registration, and the better the encoding the stronger the ultimate memory.

Memory as a Library

Your memory is very similar to a library. If that library had hundreds of thousands of books stored in it in a completely random manner, you will find it almost impossible to retrieve any one book. But if the books are stored systematically (by subject and by author for example), then retrieval becomes simple and quick.

Encoding is the equivalent of a library index. If you register each new piece of information strongly at the beginning, you will be able to retrieve (recall) it easily later. All psychologists are agreed that the better the encoding, or the more the associations, the better the retrieval.

So in evolving our Accelerated Learning system, our investigations have concentrated upon one key question - "What makes for strong encoding and for powerful associations?"

Before we turn to that, however, let us look for enlightenment from the opposite question -

"Why *do* we forget?"

The Ebbinghaus Experiments

The pioneer in memory research was Hermann Ebbinghaus who conducted the first scientific experiments on memory in Germany between 1879 and 1885.

Since he realised that meaning and associations had a powerful effect on learning, he confined himself to learning lists of nonsense syllables such as WUX, CAZ, BIJ, ZOL.

He found that there seemed an almost straight line relationship between the initial time spent in learning and the amount learned. There seemed to be neither a law of diminishing returns, nor was there a snowball effect. The more time you spent on a list the more you apparently learned. He called it the Total Time Hypothesis. It seemed to support the theory on which teaching is based even to this day - that the way to learn is through grim determination and repetition. We now know that this is simplistic - and whilst time spent is certainly important, the *way* the time is spent and the *way* the information is presented, have an enormous effect on the rate of learning. In fact, Accelerated Learning is the way to break out of the Total Time Hypothesis.

One technique will illustrate the point. Psychologists call it the "the distribution of practice effect". This shows that the time taken to learn something is significantly less if the learning is spaced out. Thus a task taking 30 minutes, if learnt all in one day, will typically take 22 minutes if spaced over two days, an almost 30% saving.

In a similar way recall is enhanced if there is a short space between two presentations of the same material. Furthermore if you test yourself and succeed in recalling the correct answer, your memory for those facts will be considerably strengthened compared with merely having the information given to you. Active involvement is always a more powerful memory enhancer than passive learning.

So a successful test is desirable. And clearly the sooner the test is conducted the higher the probability of the answer being correct.

The solution is to use the following learning strategy - which well accords to the short term/long term memory models.

TIME SCALE

Seconds	1	2	3	4	5	6	7	8	9	10
Item A	Learn/Test —		—	Test/Learn						
B			Learn/Test —		—	—	—	—	Test/Learn	
C								Learn/Test		etc

Thus you would learn (for example a new foreign word) and test (or rehearse) immediately, within the span of the short term memory. Then learn and rehearse the second item again within the Short Term Memory span. Then you would go back, after an interval, to the first item. You've achieved immediate rehearsal and also spaced practice.

The above however, has been somewhat of a digression since we are mainly interested in Ebbinghaus for his work on forgetting.

Ebbinghaus found that forgetting could be plotted on a graph - known now as the Ebbinghaus Curve of Forgetting.

The graph looks as follows:-

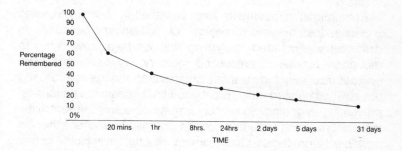

Few people will be surprised at the result.

Common experience is that memory does not seem to decay over time, but that there comes a point at which little further deterioration is experienced.

But why?

There have been two basic theories. One is that memory traces gradually fade over time rather as the sun might bleach the colour in your curtains. The other theory is that it is the number of intervening new experiences that weaken the original memory trace, "crowding out" old memories. This is called the interference theory.

Fortunately, due to a number of elegant experiments, it now seems clear that interference is the primary reason for forgetting, rather than a simple decay over time. And the more similar the events (or facts) that intervened the more that was forgotten. We might call it the Confusion Factor.

Ebbinghaus' experiments appeared to show that forgetting was an unfortunate fact of life. The more recent experiments, however, have explained the apparently inevitable memory decay as new competing experiences weakening the old memory traces. Now if that were true it would imply that the more you learnt (new) the more you would forget (old).

This is a popular misconception. Many people seem to think of memory as a water jug of limited capacity. Some of the old has to be poured out to make way for the new. As we shall see, however, the reverse is true. Your memory is more like a tree. The more branches on the tree, the greater the possibility for new branches to grow.

Ebbinghaus' experiments were designed in such a way as to produce the maximum degree of forgetting, because he deliberately eliminated everything that we have now come to recognise is vital in preserving memory. By using nonsense phrases he eliminated meaning, organisation and association, and thereby eliminated the most powerful positive factors in preventing forgetting. So his conclusions were only relevant in the most unpromising circumstances. In contrast we shall see that it is possible to create an ideal learning situation in which there is almost no forgetting.

Let us now turn from why we forget to the opposite question. What are the positive influences on memory?

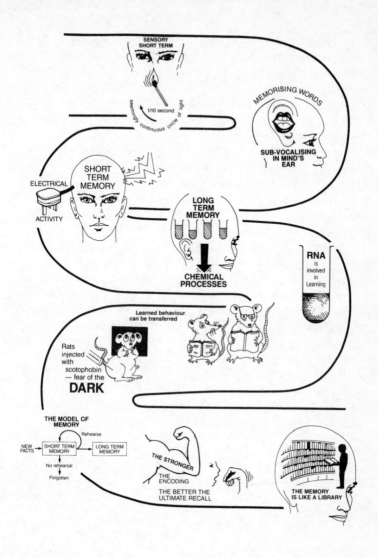

SENSORY
SHORT TERM

1/10 second

seemingly continuous circle of light

MEMORISING WORDS

SUB-VOCALISING
IN MIND'S
EAR

SHORT
TERM
MEMORY

ELECTRICAL

ACTIVITY

LONG
TERM
MEMORY

CHEMICAL
PROCESSES

RNA
is
involved
in
Learning

Learned behaviour
can be transferred

Rats
injected
with
scotophobin
— fear of the
DARK

THE MODEL OF
MEMORY

NEW
FACTS

SHORT TERM
MEMORY

Rehearse

LONG TERM
MEMORY

No rehearsal

Forgotten

THE STRONGER

THE
ENCODING

THE BETTER THE
ULTIMATE RECALL

THE MEMORY
IS LIKE A LIBRARY

39

IMPROVING MEMORY

Before we study the various positive influences on memory please indulge in a little experiment. The results will illustrate some important principles.

Test No. Two

Read through the following list once only. Read slowly and concentrate. Then look away and write down as many of the words as you recall in any order.

Grass. Paper. Cat. Knife. Love.
Bird. Tree. Desk. Truth. Table.
Fork. Pen. Stream. Wisdom. Stream.
Flower. Zulu. Radio. Ruler. Blue.
Sheep. Meaning. Field. Pencil. Carbon.

When you have written down the list of words that you have recalled, you will normally find certain things to be true. And these facts illustrate several important principles.

1. Primacy

You tend to remember more from the beginning of a test or a learning session. So you probably remembered 'grass' and 'paper'. This is called the **PRIMACY EFFECT**.

2. Recency

You also tend to remember more from the end of a learning session. So you probably remembered 'pencil' and 'carbon'. This is called the **RECENCY EFFECT**.

If you put these two effects together and plot your typical learning efficiency in memorising a list or over a period of study, say a lecture or a lesson, the effect is shown in the following figure.

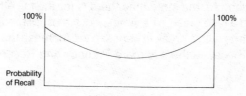

3. The Von Restorff Effect

There was probably another word that you remembered - the word Zulu. The word stood out from the list because it was different (and may have carried a quite strong visual association).

Von Restorff discovered something upon which professional memory men rely heavily. If you want to remember something, ensure it is outstanding in some way - colourful, bizarre, funny, vulgar. A bright red flower on a black dress is memorable, a subtle floral print dress may be pretty, but it is not memorable.

Outstanding elements have been measured to increase our arousal level and our attention - and you will always remember something better if it is presented in a way that either focuses increased attention, or is arousing to one or other of your senses or emotions.

Interestingly, you might also have remembered the words 'flower' and/or 'radio' which straddle 'Zulu' on the list - because the increased arousal and attention often improves recall for words or events around the original item.

By the simple expedient of inserting high recall items into a series of words, or into a lesson or lecture, you can provide a boost for attention, and therefore for encoding, retention and recall.

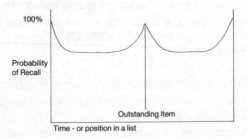

There is an interesting implication to the above. The longer the lesson or lecture, the more time there is for the fall off in attention and recall to take place. The simple device of splitting up a lesson into two parts with a break in between will increase the overall level of recall - because there is more Primacy and Recency Effect at work.

PROBABILITY OF RECALL

Specificness

If we go back again to the list of words you recalled, most people will notice that they remembered fewer of the words 'love', 'truth', 'wisdom' or 'meaning'. These words are concepts and it is more difficult to give them a concrete reality or image. In contrast, the easiest words to remember are always nouns and adjectives because they can be visualised - and as we shall see visualisation is one of the keys to memory.

For the above reasons, teaching a new language should be similar to learning your own language. Children learn the words for objects first and only later do they learn the words of abstractions like 'precedence' or 'prosperity'.

Organisation

Before we leave Test Two, have a look at the list you made. It is more than likely that you wrote the words down in clusters or groups. There were in fact several categories in the list - animals, things from the countryside, items you might find in an office, items from a kitchen and abstract concepts.

Although they were not grouped together in the list it is quite likely that you recalled them in groups.

The world famous researcher Canadian psychologist, Endel Tulving of Toronto University has conducted many experiments on the role of organisation in memory. One of the most dramatic involved two groups of students, each of whom were given 100 cards on which was a printed word. Half were instructed to *learn* the words by memorising them. The other half was instructed to sort the words out into categories.

When they were later tested the sorters or 'organisers' did equally as well as the 'memorisers' - in other words the active involvement in organising was sufficient to create learning.

43

Tulving concluded that when we try to remember something new we instinctively repeat it to ourselves. It is quite probable that it is not the repetition that is so important, as the fact that our minds are constructing associations and patterns between the words and imposing a subjective organisation on the material.

Suppose you want to remember a list of words say, - bee, pan, lamp, proud, trowel. You will more readily remember the words if you make up a sentence or sentences *connecting* the words in the form of a short story. You would remember it even better if the story was easy to visualise and best of all if you could picture a story that was dramatic, or vulgar, or comic or in some way involved your emotions.

Two more research projects emphasise the importance of *active* involvement with new material and both studies are relevant to the learning of languages.

W. Kintsch and his associates conducted an experiment in 1971 to teach three groups of subjects three new nouns. One group were instructed to read the words aloud. The second group were instructed to sort the words by type of word. The third group were asked to form *one* sentence that contained all three words. Retention of the third group was 250% better.

In the second project researchers G. Bower and D. Winzenz took four groups and required them to learn pairs of unrelated nouns.

Group 1 simply rehearsed the pairs silently

Group 2 read aloud a sentence containing the pairs of words.

Group 3 made up their own sentence and spoke them out loud.

Group 4 visualised a mental picture in which the words had a vivid interaction with each other, but said nothing out loud.

Each group performed better than the one before. The more active the involvement the deeper the learning.

The conclusions were fully validated by educational psychologists Glanzer and Meinzer who asked two groups to learn a list of new words. One group was asked to simply repeat the words six times each. The second group used the same time to think about the word and "process it mentally". The second group's recall was markedly superior.

A story is in fact a good mnemonic or memory aid and the more elaborate the story the better. A story links words to be remembered and it causes you to build up scenes that have visual, sound and sensory associations for you. Moreover the plot, however simple, provides an associative thread, so that it is normally enough to recall the theme and the *theme then triggers recall of more material.* If you can create a powerful visual image between two words, remembering one will trigger recall for the other.

Dual Encoding

The reason that a list of items learned in picture form is more easily learned than an equivalent list of printed words, is that the former are learned visually as well as verbally.

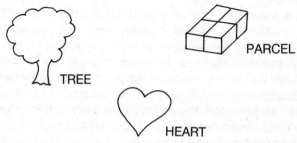

TREE

PARCEL

HEART

A picture list involves what psychologists call dual encoding - and we know that the stronger the encoding the more durable the memory and the easier the recall. In fact the ideal is not just dual but multiple sense encoding.

Principles

Consider the following sequence of letters

GNRADERECC
INELTALEA

How long do you think it would take to remember the sequence correctly? In fact you can do it in 20 seconds. By discovering the *principle* involved. Start with the last letter "A" and go up to the top line "C" across to the left "C" down to the bottom line "E" across to the left "L" up to the top "E" etc., i.e.

The sequence spells Accelerated Learning.

Similarly the following sequence 3.6.9.12.15.18.21. does not have to be memorised. You merely need to remember the principle involved. Remembering the principles involved is always more efficient than trying to remember the specifics. Chess masters can play blind-fold chess not because they recall each piece, (they don't), but because they retain the overall patterns involved.

Just how incredibly powerful this can be, is exemplified by the Belgian Master Koltanovski who in 1960 played 56 simultaneous games of blind-fold chess, winning 50 and drawing 6!

When we come to discussing the actual evolution of Accelerated Learning we shall be referring to principles, because they are a way of achieving a great deal of memory with the minimum amount of effort expended on encoding. They 'trigger' lots of recall.

In a particularly interesting study, A.S. Reber in 1967 showed that relationships between words are often subconsciously recognised. He took two groups and gave each a list of nonsense words to learn. One group had a list made up of words chosen at random - the other group had a list which was compiled according to a specific rule or principle - but that principle was not specified, it was merely implicit. The second group learned twice as well. The clear conclusion was that rules (and they include grammar) can be learnt from inference and example.

In another very simple example, taken from our own Accelerated Learning German course, we found that English learners found it difficult to remember which words were masculine or feminine or neuter. So we taught them some simple principles (or mnemonics). For example the jingle:- "height of the kite is always female", taught them in 10 seconds that all German words ending in -heit- or -keit- were feminine gender.

When we understand the principle involved - when we say "Aha, I *see* now" we have given the subject meaning and a personal relevance. We have filed it in our own particular memory - library reference file. We remember very poorly anything that is not meaningful to us, but we remember easily anything that has significance, and particularly emotional significance (Brierly 1966).

Meaning
In 1975 Craik and Tulving reported on an experiment in which subjects were asked to remember words on one of three bases.

The visual appearance of the words   (15%)
The sound of the word   (29%)
The meaning of the word   (71%)

The figures in brackets are the percentage of correctly recalled words after two presentations of the list. You will see that encoding the basis of meaning is 3-4 times stronger.

To oversimplify. You cannot become involved in something unless you understand it and it has meaning for you personally. Once it has meaning, it is capable of being associated in your mind with other words or facts you already know and understand.

If you are not 'involved' with new information it will not be processed at anything but a superficial level. It will "go in one ear and out of the other".

This is why you always remember the results of a problem that was initially difficult to solve.

Involvement then leads to a deeper processing of the material and thence to stronger memory. We have the beginning of a virtuous circle.

Context

You have probably all read the following (shortened) description). *"The first group is in. The second group go out and they try to get the first group out. Then when the first group are all out, the second group is in. The first group now goes out and tries to get the second group out. Only when both groups have been in and out twice is there a conclusion."*

An arcane passage, which would defy all understanding, unless you knew that the description was of a Cricket Match, where a team was "in" until all its batsmen had been bowled "out". So knowing the context in advance made it much easier to understand - and therefore remember.

In memorising anything it is vital to get an overview so that you understand the broad principles involved before you begin.

There is a common place parallel in everyone's life. When you visit a new country or city you look for the landmarks first and then you relate other less important places to them. You need to establish the broad geography (overview) and then systematically fill in the minor areas (detail).

This is a spontaneous and natural mapping principle, which will become significant later in this book. Educational pioneer Charles Schmid likens the importance of context to doing a jigsaw - its ten times harder if you cannot see the picture on the box.

Primitive man evolved memory largely as a way of providing himself with mental maps to record routes and the location of shelter and food. Because he had limited speech, this mapping instinct had to rely largely on an ability to visualise - bring the scene to his mind's eye. Even today primitive tribes in Africa have been shown to possess a much higher degree of visual or eidetic memory - than their Western counterparts. Eidetic memory is that ability which allows the subject to replay scenes in his or her head - almost like a video replay.

As we shall see the principle of overviewing and mapping out a subject not only provides context and, therefore, meaning but leads to the utilisation of the single most powerful element in memory - visual memory.

Physical Context

The physical environment in which you learn can also have a profound influence on your ability to recall.

The 17th Century British Philosopher - John Locke - quoted an especially odd case of a young man who had learnt to dance.

"and that to great perfection. There happened to stand an old trunk in the room where he had learned. His idea of this remarkable piece of household stuff had so mixed itself with the steps of all his dances, that though in that chamber he could dance excellently well, it was only while that trunk was there, nor could he perform well in any other place, unless that or some other such trunk had its due position in the room."

In an equally bizarre, but persuasive study, Cambridge Psychologist Dr. Alan Baddeley and Dr. Duncan Godden took a group of divers and taught them each 40 unrelated words. Half were taught under water, half were taught ashore. The words that were both learnt underwater and tested underwater were recalled almost twice as well as the words learned ashore, but tested underwater.

The implications of the fact that you recall better in the same environment, are that on-the-job training should be preferable to simulated training, and that most people learn better by learning in the same chair/desk and setting. Conversely, recalling learned material can often bring back the surroundings in which the original learning took place.

R.N. Shiffrin writing in "Models of Human Memory" proved the effectiveness of flash cards in teaching words - and found that his subjects remembered not only the word and its translation, but the size and colour of the letters and often the surroundings they were originally taught in.

Memory and Sleep

One of the major puzzles of psychology is sleep. A recent book entitled 'Landscapes of the Night', written by Chris Evans and Peter Evans, possibly represents "the state of the art" in terms of the function of sleep and dreaming.

Starting from the observation that it is, in evolutionary terms, quite amazing that mammals will risk spending a third of their lives in the highly vulnerable state of unconsciousness known as sleep, the book constructs a most realistic theory of sleep and dreaming.

Chris Evans draws an apt parallel between a human brain and a modern computer. In order for the computer to be reprogrammed it must go "off line" for some time. This is the period when new programmes are being tested and old ones modified.

In the same way the human brain needs to go "off line". The experiences of the day are reviewed during sleep and assimilated into new patterns of thought, belief, and future behaviour. This is done during the part of sleep when dreams occur. Due to investigative research by Eugene Aserinsky, working with the sleep researcher Nat Kleitman, we now know that dreams occur during paradoxical sleep (so called because the brain is in fact very active), or that portion when there is Rapid Eye Movement (or REM) sleep.

There is much circumstantial evidence that REM sleep may act as a period when the brain sorts and files new information and experiences, and decides how to adapt them. As early as 1968, Bassin concluded that *"some of the components of dreams are related to the unconscious processing of information."* If this were so, we would expect that the more new information presented during the day, the higher the proportion of sleep devoted to dreaming, i.e. REM sleep.

This turns out to be the case. Whereas adults may average 20% of their sleep in the REM sleep state this decreases as they grow older - but very young children, who are subjected to the highest proportion of new information and experiences, actually spend up to 50% of their sleep in the REM phase.

We certainly know that depriving people of sleep can have a catastrophic effect on their mental ability. In a very public demonstration of sleep deprivation, a disc jockey in New York elected to stay awake for over 200 hours. His hallucinations during the "wakeathon", started out as seeing cobwebs, rabbits and bugs and gradually became serious. He began to imagine that the room was on fire (a mysteriously common hallucination in sleep deprivation), and he began to evidence paranoia after 100 hours.

Nicholas Humphrey of Cambridge University believes that dreams act like a dress rehearsal for events we hope or fear may occur. It is as if the brain as computer, is doing a test run on a possible new programme.

Chris Evans goes so far as to say that *"we sleep in order to dream"* and the theory that these dreams are both a filing and sorting process, an assimilation of information and a series of dummy runs, coincides well with the views of Dr. Edmond Dewan, a leading sleep researcher at the Air Force Research Laboratories in Bedford Massachusetts. He notes that the lower down you go in the evolutionary scale the less the animal sleeps, and therefore can dream. *"It is almost impossible to explain the behaviour of the brain during sleep unless some re-programming is taking place".* he says.

Mothers of children will testify that during the first few days at primary school, their infants are unusually willing to go to bed. They have more novel experiences than usual to review during sleep.

REM sleep has a provable impact on memory, as you would expect. Students at Edinburgh Hospital under the supervision of Dr. Chris Idzikowsky were divided into two groups, and asked to memorise a list of nonsense syllables for 15 minutes in the morning. Half of them were tested in the evening and the other half were tested the next morning, i.e., after sleeping. The group that had slept, scored significantly higher than the first group. *"Dreams"* says psychologist Patricia Garfield *"continue work begun during consciousness"*.

It should follow that any daytime mental activity that has the deliberate intent of stimulating the subconscious, and the more visually artistically oriented right brain, should precipitate a greater review of that material during REM sleep. In turn that material should be more easily assimilated into the long term memory. Additionally, it should more easily be utilized in the unconscious creative process.

The use of sleep (or more accurately REM sleep) for creativity is well documented. One of the best known is the case of Elias Howe who invented the sewing machine. He had struggled for months to find a way to attach the thread to the needle. One night he dreamed that he was threatened by a group of natives who challenged him to invent the machine or die. As they approached him to thrust their spears into his body, Howe noticed that in the tip of the spear was a eye-shaped hole. Howe awoke instantly with the certainty that it was in the needle end that he should thread the needle.

Robert Louis Stevenson regularly willed himself to dream out the storyline and plot of his novels. He often succeeded and was really one of the first people to programme their dreams deliberately - an activity now receiving widespread attention under the name of "lucid dreaming". He actually conceived of the entire story of Jekyll and Hyde through a series of dreams.

Dr. Morton Schatzman, a psychotherapist, has had considerable success in getting students literally to "dream up" solutions to problems. In one of the simpler tests he gave a series of letters to his students. They were H, I, J, K, L, M, N, O. The letters represent a word he said. Several students reported they had dreams involving water - shark fishing, sailing, swimming, walking in heavy rain. They had subconsciously reached the solution, which was "H to O" or H_2O i.e. water.

Sleep Learning (Hypnopaedia)

If sleep helps you to assimilate facts, form opinions, reach solutions, and indulge in a "test run" of behaviour, then can you actually use the period of sleep to learn actively?

Experiments began in the U.S.A. in 1942 and extended to Russia in the 50's. "Hypnopaedia" was a popular idea but there has never been any real success with it.

On the basis of Dr. Chris Evans' work and his conclusion that sleep is when the brain, as computer, is "off line", we can understand why sleep learning has never succeeded. Learning is an activity when *fresh* information is presented. Sleep is precisely the period when the information is reviewed, not when new data are taken in.

We are now also sufficiently aware of the importance of holistic (left and right brain) learning, that we would not really expect sleep learning to work. Learning may be easiest in a state of calm, relaxed alertness, but that does not mean that you need not be fully conscious.

Taking a Break

The popular view that you need to take a break every now and then has been confirmed by French Researcher Henri Pieron. He has found that a planned series of breaks during a study period or lesson increases the probability of recall. A break every 30 minutes is probably optimum, and each break should be of the order of 5 minutes. Certainly no improvement is gained when the break exceeds 10 minutes.

The break should be a complete rest from the type of study being undertaken, otherwise too many competing or interferring associations will be formed, and they will confuse the memory traces laid down in the study period. The deep breathing and relaxation exercises - described in Chapter 12 are specifically designed to produce mental and physical relaxation and enhance oxygen flow to the brain.

The effect of the breaks will be to sustain recall in the way that the diagram opposite shows.

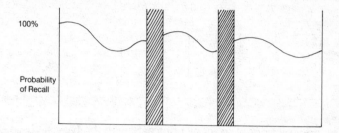

What is at work is the effect of Primacy and Recency coupled with the "Zeigarnik Effect". Zeigarnik, a German researcher, found that interrupting a task, in which a person was involved, even if that task is going well, can lead to appreciably subsequent higher recall.

Review

If breaks enhance memory consolidation, there is a similar pattern that significantly enhances long term memory consolidation, and which dramatically slashes the overall time spent in learning.

From various sources that include Tony Buzans excellent book 'Use your Head', Peter Russell's equally fascinating 'The Brain Book' and from journals of experimental and educational psychology, the following pattern of Review would seem to be ideal. It assumes that initial learning period is up to 45 minutes.

1. Learn material with immediate tests continuously built in to ensure the basic transfer from Short Term to Long Term Memory.

	Period of Review
2. Review after 10 minutes.	5 mins
3. Review after 1 day	5 mins
4. Review after 1 week	3 mins
5. Review after 1 month	3 mins
6. Review after 6 months	3 mins

This pattern of review will necessitate about 20 minutes of time per 45 minutes of initial learning, but will conservatively save many hours of learning compared with the normal instinctive urge which is to "learn it all in one go".

The pattern and its effect can be pictorialised as follows:

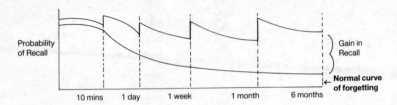

The constant boost to recall contrasts with the typical curve of forgetting we could expect with review. It would not be optimistic to expect a 400-500% boost in learning from this learning plan.

In a unique study reported in "Practical Aspects of Memory" Mangold Linton kept a diary over a four year period. She was able to show that those events in the diary which she never reviewed were 65% forgotten. Even a single review cut down forgetting significantly, whereas four reviews over a four year period reduced the probability of forgetting down to a level of about 12%. Put positively, just 4 reviews could produce an 88% probability of recall!

Your memory and your ability to learn are much, much greater than you have supposed.

Yet we have not even begun to discuss the biggest single aid to fast and effective learning - the enormous power of association. Before we do, let us turn our attention from natural actions that aid memory, to some artificial but valuable and instructive aids.

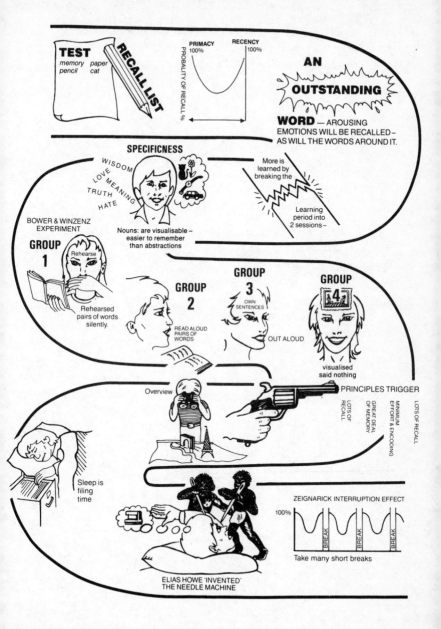

TEST

RECALL LIST

memory paper
pencil cat

PRIMACY 100%   RECENCY 100%

PROBABILITY OF RECALL %

AN OUTSTANDING WORD — AROUSING EMOTIONS WILL BE RECALLED – AS WILL THE WORDS AROUND IT.

SPECIFICNESS

WISDOM
LOVE
MEANING
TRUTH
HATE

Nouns: are visualisable – easier to remember than abstractions

More is learned by breaking the

Learning period into 2 sessions –

BOWER & WINZENZ EXPERIMENT

GROUP 1

Rehearse

Rehearsed pairs of words silently.

GROUP 2

READ ALOUD PAIRS OF WORDS

GROUP 3

OWN SENTENCES

OUT ALOUD

GROUP 4

visualised said nothing

Overview

PRINCIPLES TRIGGER

LOTS OF RECALL

GREAT DEAL OF MEMORY

MINIMUM EFFORT & ENCODING

LOTS OF RECALL

Sleep is filing time

ZEIGNARICK INTERRUPTION EFFECT

100%

BREAK   BREAK   BREAK

Take many short breaks

ELIAS HOWE 'INVENTED' THE NEEDLE MACHINE

55

MEMORY AIDS

Learning by Example

Is it better to learn a series of new words by simply learning the definition - or by example?

A rather amusing study done by K. E. Nitsch, working with researcher John Bransford at the Vanderbilt University in Tennessee, throws light on the question.

Nitsch taught his subjects some made-up words with reasonably wide potential application e.g.

MINGE - to gang up on a person or thing

CRINCH - to make someone angry by doing something inappropriate..

RELL - to rescue someone from a dangerous or problematic situation.

The question was - how well were the meanings of the words learned (by example versus by rote) and how widely could the subjects subsequently apply the new vocabulary?

The results clearly are of interest to language teaching.

The first result was very clear. The group who learned through example learned much better than those who merely recited the definitions.

The second result was obvious but significant. The narrower the context of the example, the less flexibility the student had to use the meaning in other situations. So if you teach by example - you should make the example a fairly general one.

Chunking

George Miller from Harvard University, in an influential paper entitled *'The Magical Number Seven: Plus or Minus Two'* pointed out that the immediate memory span was limited in the number of items it can hold.

He found that whether people were given lists of numbers or words, they could not correctly recall lists of more than about seven items. Now this is not surprising because it fits in with the fact that you are unlikely to sub-vocalise more than 7 items in less than 10 seconds, which is the approximate span of the short term memory store.

Miller's contribution, however, was to point out that it was the number of items that was the limiting factor - not the information contained in those items. Now, clearly, if there was only one word per item you would only remember seven words. But if each item contained quite a lot of information - or "chunks" of information as Miller termed it, - then you could increase memorisation. More information could be packed into larger chunks but not more chunks.

Chunking is, in fact, a natural process. Given a string of numbers to remember, say 4 9 3 8 6 2 7 1 2 1 you would probably reproduce it as 493-862-7121. Indeed the reason why telephone numbers are basically 7 digits in all countries, throughout the world, is that the Magic Seven is a universal phenomenon.

You will also find, that if you recite the alphabet from A-Z, you do not do so as a continuous stream, but in Chunks. Try it!

If the chunk can be rhythmical so much the better. Rhythm and rhyme are undoubted aids to memory.

Rhythm and Rhyme

A reason why monks frequently chant their prayers is because the rhythm and the rhyme are powerful mnemonics. A mnemonic being simply an aid to memory.

Another common example of the power of rhyming and rhythm is the rule -

"Thirty days has September

April, June and November."

It's chunked, it rhymes and it has rhythm. So it's well remembered.

We shall be discussing the role of music and memory in detail in Chapter 7, but most parents will be only too familiar with the ability of their younger children to remember the words of a pop song even on limited exposure, but be singularly un-impressive when it comes to a list of history dates or french verbs. The pop song is normally chunked with rhythm and rhyme, the dates are not.

Moreover the music of the pop song provides a sound and emotional association with the words - and the more associations the better encoded (remembered) is the material.

Motivation

The example of the teenager and the pop song has another significance - for there is another obvious force at work. A force that, in fact, ties together many of the points already made. We all find it much easier to succeed if we are motivated. Teenagers are motivated to 'learn' a pop song. In fact, they don't so much learn it, as absorb it indirectly. It's enjoyable and stress free. Pre-school children also learn much indirectly and it is no accident that their environment is much the same as that of a teenager absorbing a pop song.

Another virtuous circle we have found in the practice of Accelerated Learning is motivation. Since the expectation of success is high and because the pupil does indeed find learning easy and effective, the encouragement and motivation to continue fuels another round of learn/enjoy/succeed.

Children learn their own language amazingly quickly, partly because they are unconsciously using the learning principles we have rediscovered in creating Accelerated Learning, and partly because they are highly motivated to do so. It is the only way they can get what they want!

If you are motivated, if you are interested in a subject, you focus attention and that creates a climate for good learning.

It does no harm to introduce a bit of artificial motivation. Set yourself a target and, when that learning stage or task is achieved, reward yourself, in a specific manner. Buy yourself some new clothes, for example or perfume or a tie or go to a show or a meal out. The item doesn't matter - the motivation and reward does.

What about Repetition?

For all those people who have been brought up to equate learning with endless and boring repetition, we have some good news. You were right - repetition is *not* an effective way to learn!

Repetition by itself has little value unless it is accompanied by involvement.

U.S. psychologists M.J. Adams and R.S. Nickerson reporting in "Cognitive Psychology" in 1979, asked subjects to remember and draw the features of a common American coin; a coin people would expect to handle several times a day or thousands of times over a 10 year period.

The memory for the actual detail was appalling.

Equally appalling were the results of a study conducted by Dr. Alan Baddeley and Debra Dekerian at the Applied Psychology Unit in Cambridge. The B.B.C. was in the middle of a campaign to announce it was changing its wavelengths. Each subject had probably heard the announcement on her/his radio several *hundred* times. Yet correct recall was little better than guessing.

The reason why mere repetition is ineffective is not hard to guess. Firstly, without strong motivation and unless the repetition is accompanied by strong encoding, it just goes "in one ear and out the other". Secondly, the repetition itself cancels out a feature of strong encoding - the power of the unusual or outstanding to attract attention and thereby create memory.

Which brings us to the truly artificial memory aids - mnemonics

Mnemonics - The Greeks did have a word for it!

The word mnemonics is derived from the Greek "MNEME" meaning to remember and a mnemonic is anything that helps you remember better.

Many such systems exist. The first, historically, seems to have been devised by the Greek poet Simonides, following a tragedy.

Simonides was, according to Cicero, attending a victory banquet. He was called away in the middle of the festivities, just before the floor of the banqueting hall collapsed, killing and mutilating the guests and rendering many of the bodies unrecognisable. Simonides was recalled and asked to help in the identification. He found he could do so by remembering where each had sat.

From this gruesome experience he evolved the idea of visualising places in detail, in order to then remember a list of things. In clarifying the method, Cicero explained that you would first visualise a series of places about the house. (The Latin for place is 'locus' from which we get our word location).

Thus the places might be rooms in the house. Then you would visualise the objects to be remembered, placed in each room - ideally in a comical or unusual position. When the list had to be remembered, you would merely go through the places and 'see' the items in sequence.

The system was frequently used by the Romans to remember the sequence of points in a speech - hence the common phrase "In the first place" and "In the second place".

The Greeks, too, used the system and from their word 'topos' meaning place, we have derived the English "topic".

Since the nineteenth century a whole series of Mnemonic devices have been devised, and indeed marketed for sale. Most rely on the peg word system. This, too, uses visual imagery.

Peg words

This memory system is interesting for its insight into the role of visual association.

The idea allows you to remember a list of unrelated items in correct sequence. The first step is to create the 'pegs'. These have to be committed to memory by subvocalising. Because the objects rhyme with the numbers they are easy to memorise.

one	= bun
two	= shoe
three	= tree
four	= door
five	= hive
six	= sticks
seven	= heaven
eight	= plate
nine	= wine
ten	= hen

Having memorised the peg words, the next step is to relate visually the items-to-be-remembered with the correct peg word.

Supposing the second item on your list is a car. The instruction is to form a strong visual image of the car and the shoe and get that image to interact as strongly as possible. For instance, a Rolls Royce car might be parked right on top of a giant canvas shoe.

The third item to remember might be a clock. You might visualise a fruit tree growing alarm clocks instead of fruit. As you walked along you bumped your head on the alarm clock and it started to ring. This is a good interactive image because it brings in several senses. Experts in the mnemonic system stress that the more outstanding you make the image the better. It should be unusual, bizarre (remember Von Restorff?) humorous. Additionally since the mental image is entirely a private affair, you will find vulgar or sexual images make strong associations! That is because they involve the maximum number of senses.

Most readers will be familiar with the peg word memory system so we will not belabour the point. However, the principle behind the system is of the utmost importance. It involves creating a highly *visual association* between two ideas, or words or objects. The more interactive the association the better.

There are three key words in this definition of strong memory. Visual, Association and Interactive. They each bear examination.

Visual Memory

Visual images are remembered far better than words. "One picture *is* worth a thousand words".

Scientific American in May 1970 published an amazing account of an experiment conducted by Ralph Haber of the University of Rochester N.Y. Subjects were shown a series of 2,500 photographs. One every 10 seconds. Seven hours of viewing!

At the end of the session, spread over three days, the subjects were shown almost 300 pairs of photographs. One photo they had seen, the other was from a similar set of pictures, but was new.

They recognised between 85%-95% of the original pictures correctly.

In a further test subjects were presented with 600 pictures and tested immediately. They scored 98% correct! A later Canadian study conducted by R.S. Nickerson showed correct recall for vivid image pictures to be 99% correct!

For all intents and purposes visual memory can be perfect. It's a fact the advertising industry has known for years and we have incorporated it into our learning system.

Association

The brain is not like a sponge absorbing information until it eventually becomes saturated. It is a vast network of complex interconnections. Memory works in the same way.

Every new fact or concept you learn adds to and links up with the existing network. So when you encode something new, it not only forms a link to the existing network, it also provides yet another hook onto which still more associations can be hung or connected. So the more you learn and remember, the greater is your capacity for future learning and remembering.

Think back to an important joyous (or even traumatic) event in your life. You will certainly remember at least some of your surroundings at the time, or a physical sensation that went with the experience. Most people remember where they were when they heard that John Kennedy or Elvis Presley had died. Memory involves associations. If you want to create strong memory, create strong associations.

In 1972 H.R. Lindsay and D.A. Norman introduced a fascinating concept in a book called "Human Information Processing". They called it a 'Semantic Network' and it was a pictorial representation of how memory works.

From a central idea, the brain does not process thoughts in a straight line logical sequence (the left brain might, but the whole brain does not).

Instead, it brings in ideas at a tangent as connections are sparked and associations triggered. The process can be illustrated as follows:-

Let us start with a simple central idea or word........ 'Table'. The following sequence of ideas/words came to the author in the space of just thirty seconds from being given the concept of 'Table'.

The sequence was -
Table
    Chair
        Legs
            Girl
                Dress
                    Arms
                        Touch
                            Fingers
                                Spread

Freud would doubtless have been delighted with my sequence, since he first developed and regularly used the method of free association to uncover underlying sexual themes and his patients thoughts. I clearly lost no time in connecting the concept of a table and chair, via legs, to a girl. No wonder the prudish Victorians often put skirts on their tables!

The way in which this sequence of ideas or words actually developed, can be pictorialised as follows. It is a reasonable approximation of how the brain and memory typically work, forming associations and connections, some verbal, some visual, and some with both visual and action associations. Direct sensory associations - here both visual and kinaesthetic (i.e. concerned with touch), follow each other like scenes in a dream.

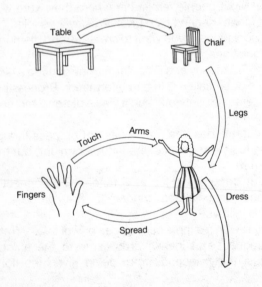

Now without going through the entire thought process, (or revealing too much of the inner workings of the authors mind!) the thirty second sequence was:-

1. **Table** - immediately associated with chair.
2. **Chair** - has **legs**
3. A **Girl** - has legs

4. A Girl often wears a **dress**
5. Mental picture of girl characteristically with **arms** held aloft as she puts on (or takes off) a dress.
6. The arms were a strong feature of the mental picture.
7. Arms are generally smooth and pleasant to **touch**
8. Touch involves **fingers**
9. Mental picture of fingers **spread** open
10. Link back to girl whose arms were spread aloft.

In just 30 seconds there were some five mental images generated and nine separate words were triggered from the original, fairly neutral word 'Table'.

If Lindsay and Norman were the first to suggest that pictorial associative networks set down ideas in the way that memory actually works, Tony Buzan has been the person most closely identified with the popularising of them as 'Mind Maps'.

We have developed even further the concept of visualising information in the same way that the brain does. We have developed what we call "Memory Maps". These act not simply as a way of revising information when it has already been learnt *but as a way of creating memory (i.e. learning) in the first place.* If information can be presented in a visual and connected form, (as was the sequence above from chair to spread), then we clearly have a device that not only incorporates visualisation, but actually and accurately reproduces the way in which the brain works. The information is predigested in the form the memory can most easily assimilate.

You will learn much more of the power of memory maps later in this book.

The Importance of Interaction

Visual images we know to be strong. But imagery can itself be strengthened if it is made to be interactive. Psychologist Gordon Bower reported on a test in which subjects were given 12 pairs of words and 8 seconds in which to learn them. Only 33% of the repeated pairs were remembered but when the subject was told to create a visual association between the pairs, the correct recall of the pairs shot up to 80%.

When the association specifically involved a direct interaction between the images, then the recall went up even further. Thus suppose the pair of words were *Dolphin* and *Flower*. An acceptable visual image would be a giant daisy floating beside the dolphin. But that brings in no *direct* connection. A better image would be a smiling dolphin blowing a stream of highly coloured flowers out of the blow hole on its head. This image has got interaction and movement and colour. The more detailed and developed the image the better.

Tests have shown that a sharp, interactive image can improve recall of word pairs by 300% compared with simple rote learning.

All this is not to imply that visual imagery is the only way of creating powerful associations and thus enduring memory. Indeed the associations involved in music (lovers often have a special song), smells (that never-to-be-forgotten whiff of perfume), and touch, can be just as powerful. But imaging by visualisation is a practical device that we can all use with no external aids. It just requires the power of our imagination.

Memory Men

Throughout history there have been people who have astonished their fellows with their apparently superhuman feats of memory. There was:-

* Mehmed Ali Halici, a Turk, who in a 1967 recording, accurately quoted over 6,500 verses of the Koran in 6 hours.

* The late Professor Aitkin of Edinburgh University who could correctly remember the first 1000 decimal places of the value of pi. It was noticeable that he 'chunked' the figures rhythmically. His achievement is now somewhat overshadowed by Hideaki Tomoyori of Japan who has memorised the first 10,000 places of pi!

* The Indian Brahmin who gives selected students special training to develop their memory. The Rig Veda is the oldest recorded work in Indo-European literature. It contains 10,550 verses and a total of 153,826 words. It is only one of four Vedas. There are students who have committed the entire sacred text to memory, in case the ancient scriptures should be destroyed.

* The Yogi Shaa, who lived in Bombay, could repeat 1,000 phrases from memory after one hearing or reading. He could reportedly memorise any poem, in any language, after hearing it just once.
* Maori Chief Kaumatara of New Zealand who recited the entire history of his tribe over 45 generations and 1,000 years to a reporter. It took three days!
* Cardinal Mezzofani, who could speak over 60 languages, most of them fluently.

All the above, and many more, demonstrate the skill of hypermnesia or super-memory. They share it with those people who have "photographic" memories. People who can recall entire pages of text and mentally run down the page until they 'see' the information they want.

The psychological term for this ability is eidetic memory. Significantly, because it seems to be a right brain capability, it occurs much more frequently in children, but decreases fairly quickly after the age of 10. There is evidence that our educational attitude, with its emphasis on logic and 'hard' facts, rather than frivolous images, may have educated eidetic memory *out* of us. Researcher E.R. Jaensch discovered that, in schools who encouraged sensory activities, a much higher proportion of children retained the clearly desirable gift of eidetic memory.

The question is, are people with hypermnesia evolutionary freaks or do they simply possess advance techniques of recall? Perhaps we are all capable of total recall?

There is some circumstantial evidence that we can.

Do we all have Photographic Memory?

At McGill University in Montreal, the now famous Wilder Penfield experiments took place between 1936-1960. A neurosurgeon, Dr. Penfield had several occasions when delicate brain surgery had to be conducted with a local anaesthetic and the patient, therefore, remained conscious. This gave the opportunity to insert minute electrodes into exposed parts of the cortex, and, by stimulating very small areas with tiny electric impulses, to note the patients' response.

When areas of the motor cortex were stimulated, the patient

would predictably show a reflex response - a twitch of a muscle or even the jerk of a limb. Smells, sounds and other physical reactions could be stimulated.

The surprise was that when the temporal cortex (above the ears) was probed, very specific memories were elicited - "as if a movie film suddenly started to roll in my head". Many, indeed most, of these memories were of apparently long forgotten and quite trivial events. A man reported seeing a comparatively unimportant friend he had not thought of, or contacted, since childhood. A woman described hearing her mother call her into the kitchen - a minor incident 30 years previously. Interestingly, even if *precisely* the same spot was stimulated more than once, the same memory was not evoked, so memory seemed not to be permanently stored in a particular spot in the brain.

These discoveries are echoed by people who have cheated death and who report that their lives flashed before them. They are reinforced by recent work with hypnotised subjects. Under hypnosis patients can recall events in much more vivid detail than they were ever conscious of assimilating in the first place.

In a fascinating series of experiments a women was regressed under hypnosis to age eight. Then she was asked to draw a picture and write a short story describing that picture.

The picture, story, and handwriting were all obviously those of a little girl. What was so remarkable, however, was that the girl's mother was able to produce an identical picture and story written in the identical style of handwriting by the same woman when she actually was an eight year old girl. The recall had been perfect after 20 years.

Other examples of recall under hypnosis are well enough known. It is quite possible to tell the number of stairs in your office or the number of panes in your lounge windows - even though you have never consciously counted them.

Police have asked accident witnesses to volunteer to give evidence under hypnosis. In the normal, conscious, state they were able to give only limited detail. Under hypnosis precise detail of colours, direction and people were recalled.

At the time these details had been subconsciously and subliminally registered, but under the right circumstances the brain can recall, not just the events on which the conscious mind was focused but the peripheral sounds and sights registered only in the subconscious mind.

A particularly impressive set of experiments has been undertaken at the Massachusetts Institute of Technology. Using a technique developed with the Bell Laboratories, subjects were exposed to pairs of Random Dot stereogram slides. Each individual slide contained a series of dots with no apparent meaning, but when they were superimposed one on top of the other, they combined to form letters, numbers or symbols.

The researchers first exposed one of the stereogram slides to the left eye. Then, later, the other stereogram was shown to the right eye. The time interval was progressively extended to as long as three days. In order to create the image, subjects had to hold in their memory the dots and their positions, so as to then later match this pattern to that of the second slide. The task required the subconscious memorisation of thousands of tiny dots.

These eidetic image stereograms could be successfully recognised by over half the respondents. Typically subjects needed about ten seconds to create the correct image. This is about the same time as the conscious mind needs to perceive subliminally embedded words in advertisements. The more relaxed the subject, the better the memory recall. However, as Professor Wilson Bryan Key points out in his excellent book, 'Subliminal Seduction', which describes the role of the subliminal in advertising, *"the perception of subliminal stimuli at the subconscious level appears to be virtually* **instantaneous and total"** (our emphasis).

Professor Key continues: *"An individual who wants to utilise a greater part of his brain-stored information, must simply learn how to move information from the unconscious into the conscious level of cognition".*

There is no known relationship between photographic memory and intelligence. The sort of regressive hypnosis we have discussed, indicates that almost anyone can recall eidetic images from any stage in their life, but that these are normally available to the subconscious and not conscious mind.

In this case the key to using the natural capacity of the brain must be to *"circumvent the conscious control systems that we erect during our formal schooling and allow the greater subconcious capacities to be used"*.

"It is quite possible", (Professor Key again), *"that the education processes of the West may be in effect, limiting man's intelligence by forcing him to repress greater and greater amounts of what he actually perceives. The implications to mankind are enormous, if individuals have innate neurological abilities vastly beyond their apparent conscious levels"*.

All this is of great significance in creating an ideal presentation for fast easy learning. The impression is being clearly formed amongst todays' psychologists that the brain, as Chris Evans put it *"has near infinite storage capacity"*. Nothing is truly forgotten. The problem seems to be not one of creating memory. We *all* have the basis of photographic memory. The problem is one of recall. The key may be in the cumbersome word Synaesthesia.

S - The Mind of a Mnemonist

If you read any text book on memory, you will certainly come across the Russian psychologist, Professor Luria. For 30 years Luria studied a most remarkable man by the name of SOLOMON VENIAMINOVICH SHERESHEVSKII, known (thankfully) as "S"., Luria published the findings of his study in a book "The Mind of a Mnemonist". "S", who was a journalist, was first sent to Luria by the editor of his paper who noticed that he never took notes - yet could repeat everything word for word.

In test after test of increasing complexity "S" showed *perfect* recall. In tests using long lists of nonsense syllables of confusing similarity - (e.g. MA.VA.NA.SA) - "S" would score perfectly, and again scored *perfect recall when tested some 8 years later!* Instructively "S" would also recall the environment of the test, the clothes Luria was wearing, the sort of day it was, etc.

The secret was his incredible capacity for visualisation and synaethesia. Synaethesia is the ability to express a memory, generated in one sense, in terms of another. Sounds expressed as colours for example.

When "S" was given a tone with a pitch of 2000 cycles per

70

second he commented -

"It looks something like fireworks with a pink-red hue. The strip of colour feels rough and unpleasant, and it has an ugly taste - rather like that of a briny pickle. You could hurt your hand on it·"

Multi-sensory imagery indeed! Whenever information was presented to "S" he encoded it in a very elaborate manner with rich associative images. The result was vivid and highly interactive imagery.

In "The Brain Book", Peter Russell quoting from Luria gives a remarkable example of how "S" remembered a complex and meaningless formula.

$$N. \quad \sqrt{d^2 \times \frac{85}{vx}} \quad \sqrt[3]{\frac{276^2.86x}{n^2v.\pi264}} \quad n^2b = sv\,\frac{1624}{32^2}\;.r^2s$$

"S" used the following imagery:

Neiman (N) came out and jabbed at the ground with his cane (.). He looked up at a tall tree, which resembled the square root sign (√), and thought to himself: "No wonder the tree has withered and begun to expose its roots. After all, it is here that I built these two houses" (d²). Once again he poked with his cane (.). Then he said: "The houses are old, I'll have to get rid of them (x). The sale will bring far more money." He had originally invested 85,000 in them (85). Then I see the roof of the house detached (————), while down below on the street I see a man playing the Termenvox (vx). He's standing near a mailbox, and on the corner there is a large stone (.), which had been put there to keep carts from crushing up against the houses. Here, then, is the square, over there the large tree (√) with three jackdaws on it (√³). I simply put the figures 276 here, and a square box containing cigarettes in the "square" (2) .. . etc.

Luria recounts how "S" was able to remember this mathematical formula in precise detail by telling the same story over 15 years later.

Of especial interest is the fact that "S" could use the same powers of visualisation or imagination to banish pain. He was able to visualise the pain as an actual shape and colour. The, when he

71

had a 'tangible' image of it in his mind, he would imagine this imaginary pain slowly easing out of his body. The real pain went with it.

In the same way he could make himself warmer by picturing himself in a hot place, or cooler by imaging himself in the Artic. But always the image was very specific and detailed and the feelings were vivid.

What is true of creating memory is of course true of learning.

Now examples like this may tempt you to think that imagination of this order is unique. It is certainly extraordinary but our imaginations *can* be trained to a higher expertise.

So the more sensory channels you can learn in, the better you will learn. Start perhaps with a visual image then link it with sounds, feelings and if possible even tastes and smells. The more the associations, the more the mental hooks on which to hang your new knowledge, and the more retrieval clues you have for fast recall when you want it.

Let's look further at the power of imagination because it is a key to Accelerated Learning. Before we do you may like to test your own powers of imagery.

Rate your power of imagery

The ability to imagine is of great importance. The following test helps you rate yourself. Just read the instruction, close your eyes and summon up the item as clearly as you can. Then use the scale to rate the clarity of the image. Note that we use the word 'image', not in a confined sense of visual image, but in the sense of conjuring up an impression that can be of smell, taste, sounds and touch, as well as sight.

Rating Scale

If the image is Very Clear you record 4 points

If the image is Clear you record 3 points

If the image is Fairly Clear - record 2 points

If the image is Unclear you record 1 point

If the image is Non-existent - record 0 points

72

When you have tried all the instructions add up the points and check with the rating scale at the end.

1. See yourself throwing a ball
2. Imagine yourself smelling some lavender
3. Picture the house you grew up in
4. Picture a close relative standing in front of you
5. Picture a friend looking worried
6. Imagine a black forest gateaux
7. Picture the eyes of a close friend
8. Imagine the first few bars of your favourite song
9. Imagine the feeling of the hot sun on your skin
10. Imagine the texture of coarse sandpaper
11. Picture a kettle boiling
12. Imagine a cold wind when its raining
13. Picture yourself riding a bicycle up a steep slope
14. Hear a factory siren
15. Picture a South Sea island
16. Picture the room in which you work
17. Imagine the smell of new mown hay
18. Feel yourself picking up a heavy object
19. Feel the warmth of a hot bath
20. Picture a favourite article of clothing

Rating Score

If you scored 60 or more, your power to image is very good

If you scored 31-59 your power to image is good and can be improved even further by imagery techniques.

If you scored 30 or less you will obtain great benefit and pleasure from the imagery training we describe later.

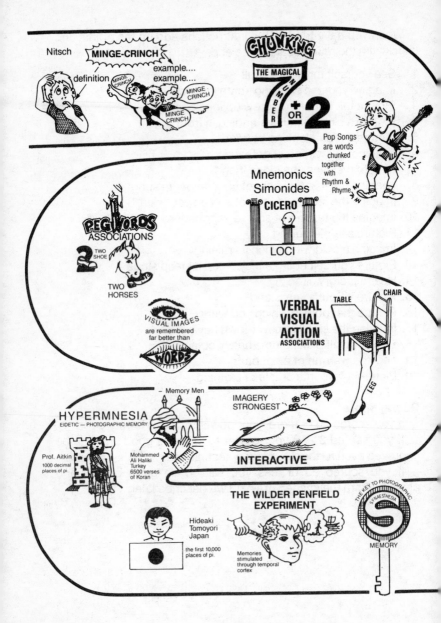

74

THE POWER OF YOUR IMAGINATION

Prologue

Imagine you are in the kitchen. You take a fresh lemon from the fruit bowl. It is cool in your hand. The yellow dimpled skin feels smooth and waxy. It comes to a small green conical point at either end. The lemon is firm and quite heavy for its size as you look at it in the palm of your hand.

You raise the lemon to your nose. It gives off such a characteristic, unmistakable citrus smell doesn't it? You take a sharp knife and cut the lemon in half. The two halves fall apart, the white pulpy outer skin contrasting with the drops of pale lemon coloured juice that gently ooze out. The lemon smell is now slightly stronger.

Now you bite deeply into the lemon and let the juice swirl around your mouth. That sharp sour lemon flavour is unmistakable.

Stop a minute! Is your mouth watering? Did your mouth pucker? If it is, you have achieved synaesthesia, because you imagined the feel, sight, smell and taste of the lemon. You have used your imagination well. The implications are fascinating, because of course, nothing actually happened - except in your imagination! Yet your mind communicated directly to your salivary glands and told them to wash away the sour taste.

The words you read were not reality - but they created reality - your flow of saliva. *The subconscious mind cannot differentiate between what is real and what it believes is real.*

Yet it directly controls your actions in a very tangible way.

There's Nothing Good or Bad but Thinking Makes It So
(Hamlet)

"Man freezes to death in refrigeration car". The 1964 headline was hardly startling, but the circumstances were. A man had become trapped inside the refrigeration car as the door accidently slammed on him. When he was found, he had all the physical symptons of having frozen to death. Yet the refrigeration unit was switched off and at no time had the temperature been at, or even close, to freezing. He believed he was going to freeze - and his mind had produced the physical effect to create hypothermia and freeze him to death.

A man lay quietly in an Haitian hut, resigned to the inevitability of death. He had seen the voodoo doll in his likeness with pins stuck in it. In reality he was perfectly healthy, but his mind had accepted the inevitable, and he had subconsciously willed himself to die. Only the intervention of a priest, who destroyed the doll in front of him, saved the Haitian's life.

Researcher Dr. Cheureul spoke quietly to his subject, who was holding a pendulum over a straight line on a piece of paper. *"Keep it as steady as you can,"* he instructed, *"although you will find that the pendulum is bound to swing up and down the line because of the earth's gravitational pull".*

After a few minutes the pendulum began to swing quietly - although the reason Cheureul gave was absolutely bogus. There was no reason for the pendulum to swing - other than the subconscious suggestion that it would.

The above instances are all examples of self fulfilling prophesies brought about by suggestion. There are thousands more.

Children invited into the New York University's Department of Psychology were assessed according to the wealth of their parents. They were then asked to estimate the physical size of a group of coins. The poorer children ALL over-estimated the actual size, the richer ones ALL under-estimated the real size.

Dr. Rosenthal, a California psychologist, administered I.Q. tests to a public school class. He totally ignored the results, but nevertheless divided the class into two groups. The first group, he informed the teacher, was considerably brighter than the second. There was, in fact, no difference. The children were never told his conclusions and the teacher was told to treat all the pupils the same.

Eight months later the grades of the two arbitrarily classified groups were compared. The first group had grades 28% better than the second group and their I.Q.'s actually measured higher! Without one word being said, the teacher had managed to communicate, quite unconsciously, a higher expectation of the first group and a lower expectation of the second group. ALL WITHOUT THE SUBJECTS EVEN KNOWING. The teacher had created a better learning environment for the favoured group, and it worked.

Students in a Bulgarian class were asked to memorise a poem. Another identically matched class was also asked to memorise the same poem, but this time they were told the author - who was a famous and respected poet. The second group remembered 60% more than the first group, in the same time period. The authority of the author suggested it was important to learn.

We act not according to what things really are - but according to what we expect them to be: believe them to be: imagine them to be.

"Imagination," said Napoleon, *"rules the world"*.

He should have known, for he actually rehearsed every battle he ever fought weeks before the event in his mind. Going over his own tactics, visualising the enemy defences, their reaction and the terraine.

Napoleon was 150 years ahead of his time.

Jack Niclaus ascribes his success to visualisation. Before every shot, he actually "sees" the club strike the ball, watches the flight of the ball in the air and "sees" where it comes to rest - all before he actually makes the shot. Top tennis pro's do it. *"Golf is 90% mental, 10% mechanical."* wrote Alex Morrison the father of modern golf teaching. The same can be said of many other sports and the visualisation technique is now widely known as the "Inner Game of Tennis".

Inner Sports

Tim Gallwey in his best selling book "The Inner Game of Tennis", showed how visualisation can be much more effective than verbal instruction. As a tennis Pro, he became aware that each pupil's mind seemed to contain two entities. A Self 1 who observed and commented on the play, and a Self 2 who actually did the playing.

Before a shot Self 1 would issue all sorts of commands such as "keep your eyes on the ball", "bend your knees", "follow through".

Then, after the shot, would come a verbal analysis - usually critical. When asked why they did this, most players would respond, "I am just talking to myself".

Gallwey rationalised that "I" and "myself" had to be two separate entities, otherwise no conversation would take place. He developed the theory that Self 2 would be better taught by non-verbal means, and that the "relationship" between Self 1 and Self 2 must be improved to optimise performance. Indeed he observed that an athlete's peak performance usually occurred when the verbal Self 1 was almost totally set aside. Players on a "hot streak" almost never analysed what they were doing - they were immersed in the physical action and played instinctively and unconsciously. As soon as they tried to exercise conscious control, they lost their fluidity.

Gallwey, therefore, taught his players to engage, or distract, the verbal Self 1 during play, by describing external events. They would say "bounce" when the ball bounced, or "hit" when it struck the racket. They alternatively would be told to say the words of a song. These distractions, left brain activities, allowed the right brain and limbic system to control the physical play and make all the highly complex intuitive calculations that are involved in assessing ball speed, direction and angle of bounce.

The importance of not over-analysing and of not verbalising an essentially non-verbal activity, was further re-inforced when 'Inner Skiing' was introduced. Small children, it was noticed, could learn to ski well in a day. Adults learn (or are taught) to depend more and more on verbal analysis and to trust intuition less and less.

The inadequacy of the verbal hemisphere controlling the subtle but essentially physical movements of skiing, is made all too obvious when you observe the jerky movements made by people who are clearly rehearsing their instructors words in their minds. The fluent skier very often cannot even describe how he or she does it - yet obviously knows on a non-verbal level. Consequently increasing emphasis has been put on teaching ski-ing in non-verbal ways - and the positive results can be dramatic.

The Placebo Effect

It is well known that physicians regularly use placebos - sugar pills or pills with absolutely no real medical power. The patients, however, are told that the pills are powerful medicaments. Countless studies have proved the high effectiveness of these "mind only" medications.

In a 1979 study, patients with severely bleeding ulcers were split into two groups. One was told that they were taking a new drug that would bring immediate relief. The second was told that they were taking an experimental drug, but not much was yet known about its effects. The same drug was administered to both groups. 75% of the first group improved - 25% of the second group. The only difference was the patients' expectations.

At Harvard University Dr. Beecher researched pain in post operative patients. Some were administered morphine and some a placebo. The morphine controlled the pain in 52% of the patients who received it - the placebo controlled the pain in 40% of the patients. In other words the placebo was 75% as effective as the morphine. The brain, expecting the pain relief, actually triggered the production of endorphins, the naturally produced opiate chemicals that block the neurotransmitters which allow the sense of pain to register on the brain.

Mind over matter

Many researchers are now convinced that a good proportion of the benefit derived from real medication is received from the placebo or "halo" effect. Since everyone, including the doctor, knows that extensive testing goes into new drugs, when one is released for use, the doctor expects it to work, the patient expects it to work - and it does work.

A placebo works because the subconscious mind finds ways of bringing about what you imagine, and believe, will happen.

Because of the undoubted power of the mind to produce healing, or indeed sickness in the patient, doctors worldwide are more and more moving towards holistic medicine. Holistic merely means (W) holistic - treating the *whole* patient - not just his body, but his mind too.

In one of the most dramatic proofs of the power of mental attitude over recovery rates, 152 cancer patients at the Travis Air Force base in California were rated by their doctors, as to whether they had a positive or negative expectation of recovery. Without exception the patients with positive expectations had far more successful remission rates. In fact only 2 out of the negative attitude patients showed any response to treatment at all. So much so that the physician in charge was able to state that . . .

"A positive attitude towards treatment was a better predictor of response to treatment than was the severity of the disease."

The above examples all illustrate the power of the imagination to suggest behaviour and attitude changes. In some instances that power was brought about by auto suggestion - the mind voluntarily created its own reality. In other instances the suggestion was from an external source. Someone had "put the idea in the subjects' head·"

Is there a limit to the power of the mind over the body?

Probably not.

Doctors Elmer and Alyce Green are pioneers of biofeedback research at the Menninger Clinic in Topeka, Kansas.

"Bio-feedback" merely means that the subject of the experiment receives a physical signal - a dial reading, a musical note or the flash of a light - to indicate whether they have succeeded in producing a physical response. Thus patients have been taught to voluntarily slow down their heart rates. As their pulse began to slow in response to mind calming exercises, they were told to expect to hear a deeper and deeper note on their earphones. That signal of success itself enabled them to slow the heart rate further - so the tangible result of their efforts "fedback" a signal that produced another round of relaxation, and hence another signal of success. So bio-feedback is merely a psychological/physiological technique, known more popularly as "success breeds success", or as we term it - creating a "virtuous circle".

Using this technique the Greens have been able to train a subject to cause extra blood to flow to one earlobe and not the other, thus selectively raising the temperature of that earlobe! They have trained subjects to control almost all the functions previously termed "involuntary" responses - heart rate, muscle tension, even sweat gland activity.

The technique of course, is well known in Eastern cultures and advanced Yogis have been scientifically measured as capable of slowing their breathing rate down from 20 times per minute to as low as 2 per minute.

In a recently published study from the Menninger Clinic the Greens reported experiments where subjects had learned to control, with their minds only, *A SINGLE NERVE CELL,* a feat equivalent in its accuracy to the current limits of micro surgery.

The same research team were able recently to correlate an increased level of Alpha & Theta brainwaves with a substantial acceleration in the acquisition of new knowledge.

Hypnotism

The power of mind over body is indeed astonishing.

In the Psychology Department of a London experimental hospital a woman had been hypnotised. The hypnotist touched her arm with his fingers and said quietly, "That's a red hot poker" Not only did she flinch with pain, but her lymphatic system caused an immmediate red weal to appear on her arm.

In another experiment an all-in heavy-weight wrestler was seated at a table. The red light of the T.V. camera was on and the whole scene was video taped. The hypnotist told the wrestler that the pencil in front of him was stuck to the table and that he would not be able to lift it. The wrestler, who could lift 300 lbs in a straight overhead lift, strained and the muscles of his neck stood out - but he literally could not lift the pencil. The suggestion had caused his muscles to contract, and there was no strength available in his arm.

In a directly opposite experiment the gripping strength of an athlete had been measured on a dynometer and registered as 100 lbs. In test after test this was his maximum. Under hypnosis he was told "You are much stronger than you have ever been. You are surprised at how much stronger you have become".

Again he was tested, and now the needle swung smoothly through the 100 lbs 'barrier' and registered at 125 lbs.

This time the hypnotist had removed the athlete's mental block that his strength was limited to 100 lbs. *The hypnosis worked not by adding actual strength, but by removing a self imposed and limiting belief about himself.*

Norris McWhirter, editor of the world famous Guinness Book of Records, states that there never was a 4 minute mile 'barrier'. It was all in the minds of the athletes and when it was eventually smashed, scores of athletes quickly followed Roger Bannister's breakthrough. The real limit, says McWhirter would come at around 3.36 when the runners' body would overheat so much that the brain would automatically cut off all forms of physical effort.

In this sense many 'cures' under hypnosis are really the effect of 'dehypnotising'. They work by taking away the self suggestion that something cannot be done. When a stammerer is cured, an arithmetical 'dunce' multiplies two three figure numbers in his head, it is all because the hypnotist has removed a negative expectation from their mind.

In a long series of experiments Prescott Lecky, an American educational psychologist, who had previously worked as a full time teacher, became convinced that a negative self image was the key reason why individual students learnt slowly. For such students to learn quickly, Lecky theorised would be contrary to their self image. But if you changed the self image, you could change the learning ability.

It worked. A student with an average of 55 misspelt words out of 100 improved to 91% within six months. A Latin student with 30% grades, achieved 84% after just three positive talks with a sympathetic teacher. A student who had been written off in his end of term report as having "no aptitude for English" won the literary prize the very next term!

None of these students, or the hundreds of others whom Lecky counselled, had any lack of intrinsic ability. What they did lack was positive self image.

They were told by comment or by their early works that they were poor spellers or poor mathematicians; and they came to believe it.

Instead of accepting that they had failed a test, or made a mistake, they had come to generalise that one failure into the overall subconscious conclusion that "I am a failure". All too quickly a failure in one or two early arithmetical tests can become internalised into "I am no good at maths".

What is the difference between Suggestion and Hypnotism?

The last few examples have, quite deliberately, been mixed between suggestion (the four minute mile "barrier") and hypnotism (the wrestler who could not lift a pencil).

Where does suggestion end and hypnotism begin or are they quite different?

Suggestion is an integral part of every single piece of day to day communication. If a Nobel prize winner, dressed in a sober suit, announced an amazing new technical breakthrough at a scientific conference, you would be more inclined to believe it than if you were told by a scruffily dressed stranger in a pub. The medium, to paraphrase Marshall McLuhan, is part of the message.

In all communication, the tone of voice of the speaker, the movement of his hands, his dress, your knowledge of his background, all suggest information to you over and above the content of his message. Sometimes the subconscious or subliminal impressions or suggestions reinforce your understanding and memory of the content upon which your conscious attention is focused. At other times subliminal, or peripheral suggestions contradict the message.

Patricia Durovy of the American Society for Training and Development estimates *"90% of all communication is subconscious"*. It could be an underestimate.

Although suggestion works very powerfully indeed at the subconscious level, the conscious mind generally continues to act as a censor. It will normally reject suggestions that do not accord with our moral values, or with logic, or that threaten our sense of confidence and security.

The key difference between suggestion and hypnotism is that suggestion, can and does, bring the power of the subconscious to bear, but without relinquishing the censor role of the conscious mind. Under hypnotism you are partially relinquishing control of both your conscious and unconscious mind to someone else. Moreover, suggestion can bring about permanent changes in ability and behaviour, whereas, hypnotism is normally intended to focus on a temporary state - though it can, of course, have excellent long term therapeutic results.

Interestingly, hypnotism has great similarities with sleep. Many of the brain-wave patterns are very similar, and both involve reduced conscious control.

Suggestion can have very positive and measurable results. An Oklahoma anaethetist Mrs Jean Mabry regularly waits until her patients are under anaethesia and whispers encouraging and positive instructions to them. Consultant surgeons working in her report markedly improved recovery rates.

Imagination and Suggestion

Although it is easy to use the words imagination and suggestion interchangeably, there is an important distinction between them.

Imagination is the ability to visualise to produce a mental impression of sights, sounds, smells, tastes and memories of touch. You can use imagination to create a strong visual link between two ideas you are trying to remember. Used in this way, it is a key to memory.

However, imagination is also needed to create a suggestion, and suggestion can bring about a permanent and far reaching change in your attitudes and capabilities.

Some 20 years ago a research psychologist at the University of Sophia realised, that the power of suggestion could be used to improve teaching methods.

His name was Georgi Lozanov and his work, and the highly successful learning method to which it led, provided the initial impetus for this book.

I first heard of Georgi Lozanov from an exciting book called "Super Learning". The book made the bold claim that Lozanov had evolved a teaching method that would improve learning effectiveness and increase the speed of learning by from 3 to 10 times. A Japanese had learnt English in 10 days. Students at the University of Iowa had learnt a year of Spanish in 3 months. Complete beginners had learned 900 words French *in a day*. The book was full of claims of better, faster learning.

Inevitably, I was initially sceptical, but I felt, that even if it were only partly true, something of great importance had been developed.

So I flew to New York to meet the two co-authors of 'Super Learning', Sheila Ostrander and Lynn Schroeder.

They turned out to be journalists of intelligence and integrity. I was convinced they were reporting events exactly as they saw them, but I felt I needed to see Lozanovs' method for myself - and above all to understand *why* he achieved such astonishing results.

The next chapters describe what we discovered. They give the documentary proof that Lozanov's methods do indeed work.

We have spoken with the Educational Departments of four Governments, leading University psychologists and professional educators, in order to discover *why* Lozanov methods worked. As we did so, we began to sense that something exciting and important was happening. It was clear that Georgi Lozanov had indeed evolved a "super-learning" method, but that there were also areas in which it could be significantly improved. Moreover, those improvements were being built into a learning method that could be used by anyone, of any age, and in any learning situation. The method evolved by a group of gifted psychologists and teachers, has become known as Accelerated Learning and it has been adapted successfully for home study courses.

The start point is to review the work of the founder of this revolutionary learning movement - Georgi Lozanov.

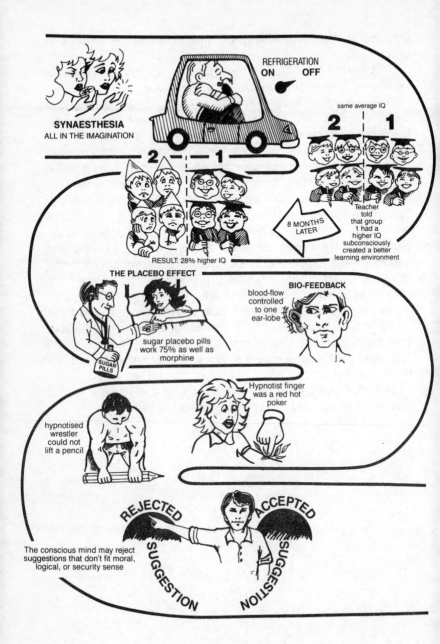

SYNAESTHESIA
ALL IN THE IMAGINATION

REFRIGERATION
ON OFF

same average IQ

2 | 1

Teacher told that group 1 had a higher IQ subconsciously created a better learning environment

8 MONTHS LATER

2 | 1

RESULT: 28% higher IQ

THE PLACEBO EFFECT

sugar placebo pills work 75% as well as morphine

SUGAR PILLS

BIO-FEEDBACK

blood-flow controlled to one ear-lobe

Hypnotist finger was a red hot poker

hypnotised wrestler could not lift a pencil

REJECTED SUGGESTION   ACCEPTED SUGGESTION

The conscious mind may reject suggestions that don't fit moral, logical, or security sense

THE GENESIS OF ACCELERATED LEARNING

Dr. Georgi Lozanov is Bulgaria's leading research psychologist. A medical doctor, he is now renowned for the breakthrough in education theory that led to Accelerated Learning.

Dr. Lozanov obtained his PhD for his work on the application of suggestion in the field of medicine and education. For his doctorate he spent months investigating the phenomenon of hypermnesia - photographic memory. He worked with people who had extraordinary mental powers - from a Russian who could multiply four figure numbers faster than a computer, to Indian mystics who could remember 10,000 verses word-perfectly. His conclusions and theories were built into a learning system that is radically different from any other.

The learning system that is now in daily use in hundreds of classrooms across Eastern Europe, the United States and Western Europe, is, of course, very different from the prototype developed in 1956 at the University of Sophia. The principles, however, have remained constant, even when translated from the Bulgarian culture to, for example, the United States.

When you walk into a Lozanov method class, you walk into a very different environment from that which most people associate with teaching. Let me describe a lesson we attended at the Lozanov Learning Institute in Washington.

A dozen people sit in comfortable reading chairs in a semi circle around the teacher. Behind him are the twin speakers of a large stereo music centre.

On the walls are colourful pictures of animals and familiar objects with the Spanish words for that object lettered faintly across them.

The teacher is master trainer Peter Kline. He smiles and announces that the method the class will use in learning Spanish is the method by which a test group of disbelieving visitors from

UNESCO (United Nations Education and Scientific Cultural Organization) learned to recognise 1,200 new words of a foreign language in a single day!

The Lozanov method, says Kline, involves six main principles:-

one We have to de-suggest the idea that your ability is limited. To remove the negative mental blocks that cramp our natural learning ability. Those self-imposed limitations are a cultural legacy and paradoxically are produced by our school system! In place of these artificial limitations, we put the powerful and positive suggestion that learning is in reality easy, fun and enjoyable.

two We relax - because we know that relaxation creates the ideal condition of stress-free alertness, when information is rapidly and effortlessly absorbed.

three We create a mental map of the information we are going to learn. In the case of a language we go over the entire lesson first in English, so we know the story and what to expect and to provide a context we can relate to. Then we read it in Spanish to get the feel of it.

four We hear what is known as the "Active Concert". This is a reading of the Spanish text in a dramatic manner to the accompaniment of a specific type of classical music as a background. The music is mostly by Baroque composers like Corelli, Telemann, Haydn, Bach, Albinoni and Vivaldi. Music composed between 1700-1750.

The teacher's voice follows the rhythm of the music in a natural way - as if his voice were an instrument in the orchestra.

We follow the sound of the language and look at the words in a unique text book. The words are so laid out, that even while the eye is following the Spanish text, the English translation is in the peripheral vision of the reader - in other words he is subconsciously taking in both texts - the Spanish consciously, the English subconsciously, out of the "corner of his eye".

"This", explains Peter Kline, *"is one of the visual subliminal elements. The music is the main audio route into the subconscious. We find we can access the further reaches of the*

subconscious better through art, because art involves the emotions. Harmony of form and colour music and rhyme, reach not only the heart but the mind - via a much shorter route than logical facts and arguments."

In fact the music works by activating the right brain and in this way the left and right brains are directly and independently stimulated. Sound and visual stimuli, your conscious and subconscious, "Super-liminal" and subliminal stimuli, are each involved to speed the information into the memory in a positive and enjoyable environment.

The brain is known to store information in a rhythmical way, so the use of rhythm as an external aid is entirely logical.

Bio-feedback expert, Dr. Budzynski, writing in "Psychology Today" confirmed Peter Kline's point -

"Apparently the right hemisphere processes verbal material better if it is coded in rhythm or emotion. When someone speaks in a monotone, only the verbal, dominant hemisphere is activated. If the speaker adds intonation, the nonverbal side starts to pay attention. The right hemisphere's language is not the logical content of what is said, but the emotions conveyed by how it is said. Lecturers, preachers, and politicians who are famous for the oratory know intuitively what to do with their voices to generate emotion and thereby persuade their audiences".

The medium is the message.

five   After the Active Concert there is a break. Then the Receptive Concert takes place. It is so called because it requires that the student apparently makes no effort at all. In reality, however, an enormous amount of mental activity is taking place. Before the Receptive Concert the students are told "Relax in your chairs, close your eyes and just concentrate on the music". Now the music becomes the dominant factor and the words of the Spanish text are only just audible to the conscious mind. They are, however, perfectly understandable to the subconscious and thus the barriers of the conscious mind are neatly side stepped.

"The purpose of the receptive concert," says Peter Kline, "is to give you a familiarity with speech as normally used in the language you are studying - its patterns and natural rhythms. You are relaxed, and the music creates an ideal mental state (alpha) for an effortless absorbtion of the material.

"The whole of the first lesson will bring about a co-ordination of left and right brain, in a synthesis that creates a quantum leap in learning speeds and retention." "Just how much of a leap?" asks a student. Peter Kline answers that every Western Application has shown a significant gain in learning - from minimum of trebled learning effectiveness to as much as ten times faster. *"Expect a four fold increase"* smiles Kline *"and you will be pleased at your results."*

The class ends after a total of two hours. The posters and cards around the room have, again subconsciously, reinforced the lesson.

The next day begins with the sixth and final main element.

six   After the deliberate intervention of a night's sleep, the next day's class starts with what is termed the Activations.

These consist of a series of games, puzzles, and playlets devised to review the words learned the previous day, in an environment that is fun and deliberately childlike. Lozanov insists that a key to the method is to return to the way children learn before they go to school. It's not only stress free, it's characterised by high expectations of success. Mistakes, if they occur, are taken, *correctly* as a sign that the learner is deliberately stretching herself with new material. It's a sign of ambition and lack of fear.

One game that particularly impressed me used a ball! The teacher would throw the ball to the student to catch and simultaneously ask a question in Spanish. The students answered spontaneously as they caught the ball. Time after time they exclaimed *"I was surprised I knew the words of the answer. They just popped up."* In fact the teacher was deliberately distracting the student's conscious attention by the act of catching the ball - and allowing the words, which were already stored in the subconscious, to surface. It was impressive proof that the memory had indeed already been created.

The thinking behind the second day's Activation session is that the intervening night's sleep and dreaming will have allowed the brain to assimilate the new words. The next day review ensures that they are then 'fixed'.

One cannot help but be impressed at the way everything in these Lozanov classes is co-ordinated to bring about "learning in the round".

The storyline of the lessons is dramatic because dramatic facts and stories with emotional associations are more easily remembered.

The pictures in the text book are expertly drawn because as Peter Kline points out "art aids suggestion". Additionally, individual pictures have the Spanish word lettered into the outline of the drawing. A picture of a lion for example has the word "leon" lettered into it.

Each student is assigned a Spanish name and character. It becomes a role to play. The theory is that when the student makes a mistake he makes it "in the name of his new Spanish alter ego". Consequently, the mistake is transferred to the new character, and does not in any way reflect on the student himself.

It is also noticeable that every single element of the class is positive. No criticism. Just encouragement. It is the sort of supportive atmosphere that a child normally learns in. Everything was focused to ensure effective stress free learning. Words, pictures and sound were all co-ordinated. Left brain/right brain activity was co-ordinated. Conscious/subconscious influences were co-ordinated.

The childlike joy of learning was married to the adult's store of prior knowledge.

The Lozanov method is holistic learning at a very refined level.

I asked Peter Kline what he felt was the secret of the method's success. I had already been told the facts of the success. Students normally learnt a language in a month, a seven times speed up in learning. A 'norm' was to be able to recognise hundreds of new words a day, at 90% retention.

How was it done? His answer was revealing.
"Children learn spectacularly well up to the age of 5. They

expect to learn. Everything is fresh, stimulating, exciting and easy. Children essentially teach themselves. From a sea of information that surrounds them, they pick out the pieces that interest them at the moment.

"They gradually build up a structure in their minds of how their own language works. They figure out the grammar for themselves. Vocabulary is built up as phrases in the context of a real life situation. No one gives them rules or lists of nouns.

"Then the learning curve falls rather dramatically. A funny coincidence. People are presented with information in a very different manner from how they learnt pre-school. How can they come into the world knowing absolutely nothing and learn a natrive language? With 100% success? With nobody teaching them in a formal way. Study that and you'll figure out the Lozanov method".

That gave me pause for thought. Play *is* central to learning. It is a way of acting out things we need to explore. It is perhaps the daytime equivalent of dreaming. A dress rehearsal without the tension of the "serious" performance?

Children have fabulously creative imaginations. They are constantly exposed to new ideas so that their imagination is continuously stimulated. Yet as they grow older their innate ability to conjure up impressions and to remember seems to decline, in inverse proportion to their ability to reason in a logical manner.

The more we are taught the logical relationships between things, the "laws" of science or behaviour, the fewer the childlike leaps of imagination. We no longer feel so vividly - we concentrate on the maps, forgetting the countries they represent. The development of step by step logical thought patterns (left brain emphasis), seems usually to reduce the capacity to imagine vividly (right brain capability) and hence remember vividly.

A characteristic of children is their spontaneity, open mindedness and high expectation of enjoyment. It is an environment worth recapturing.

Kline encourages the expression of emotion in the classes - "You can't separate the intellectual from the emotional. In fact an emotional content to learning makes it easier to remember because people remember more in a higher state of arousal. The key to what we are doing is to distract the conscious mind and *'click' the information in when you're not looking!"*

The introductory remarks that Peter Kline made in the lessons I visited, were completed by a videotape of one of the early Lozanov classes at his Institute in Sophia. The video was officially produced by UNESCO, who have welcomed the technique as an important advance in education. The following description of this film is taken verbatim from the North West Orient Magazine because it captures the flavour of the video tape so well.

"As the video tape begins the viewers see about a dozen, stiffly formal, male Russian government officials in sombre suits file into a classroom for their first exposure to French. From the outset the short, lithe woman who is the Lozanov instructor, speaks only in French and dramatises outrageously everything she says. The men sit like boulders as she acts out a lesson. Occasionally they glance nervously out of the corners of their eyes at each other.

The tape progresses to a time a few days later. The men are now in shirtsleeves and have begun to have a playful look about them. The instructor asks one question in French and throws him in inflated plastic ball. He answers in French and throws it back. By the next sequence, a few days later, the men are all marching around the room after the instructor, swinging their arms back and forth exaggeratedly and singing a French song.

Finally, the men have had enough French instruction and are ready to initiate their own conversation. The tape advances further and suddenly we see one of the men on a stage pretending to be coming home for dinner. He issues a greeting in remarkably well accented French and the greeting is returned by another of the men, who is playing the first man's wife and is dressed in a short skirt, a blouse and a bandanna and is holding a plastic doll. Some spirited discussion ensues in fluent French, the gist of which seems to be (to the unschooled observer) that dinner is not ready. Why is dinner not ready? Because I spent all day taking care of the baby! The drama goes on, most remarkable for the fact that, not only are these men arguing in French, when they had no knowledge at all of it merely weeks previously, not only are they moving with great animation across the stage, when formerly they sat like stones, not only are they acting with the abandon of small children, but above all they all are immensely enjoying themselves.

There's something tremendously refreshing about the whole scene."

After the video tape ends, Peter Kline chose his words carefully, *"Conventional language teaching is unnatural because the entire situation is artificial. The rigid and pedestrian progress from apparently easy words, to "more difficult passages" implicitly emphases that you can expect everything to get more difficult. Since you expect things to get more difficult, they do!*

"Our techniques," he says, *"mirror the child like learning process. You pick up the language and construct the structure for yourself.*

"It's global teaching rather than piecemeal teaching.

"It requires you to dive in, initiate things, make mistakes, experiment. It's fun and will improve your general creative ability.

"It never gets more difficult than in Lesson 1.

"It's a holographic approach, not a linear approach - so if you don't figure out the way the language is constructed in Lesson 1 you can do so in Lesson 3 or 5, or whenever you're ready.

"Each new word is introduced in such a way that is meaning is made clear by the context in which it appears. Words are re-used often enough so that they quickly become familiar. Many more words of text are used to introduce new vocabulary than is customary in other foreign language courses.

"Thus one can relax and allow the brain to become familiar with the sounds of the words and gradually absorb their meaning. This is directly comparable to the way in which a child is exposed to its language. He gradually associates familiar sounds with meanings.

"In traditional learning a source of tension is fear of the unknown. An unfamiliar word becomes a threat. In this approach you are secure all the time because the meaning of the word is always immediately available."

In all, I and my colleagues, spent several weeks at the Lozanov Institute in Washington with founder Carl Schliecher and with Peter Kline. We came away personally convinced that it worked. We had seen the students, their enthusiasm and their success.

But we are troubled by a number of questions.

1. How important is the music, and how does it work in the context of a Lozanov Accelerated Learning Course?

2. Where was the objective evidence and if the method worked so well, - why weren't more people using it. In fact, why wasn't everyone using it?

3. Our current educational system may not be perfect but surely they can't be accused of actually teaching us to accept we have less potential than we really have?

4. We were aware that great advances had been made in the last decade in understanding the brain and memory - did these developments validate Lozanov? Or could they be used to evolve an even better system?

The answers to those questions took three years to compile and involved visits to twelve countries but we are finally convinced we have a learning method that can benefit everyone, adult or child.

Let us look at those questions and the answers we found.

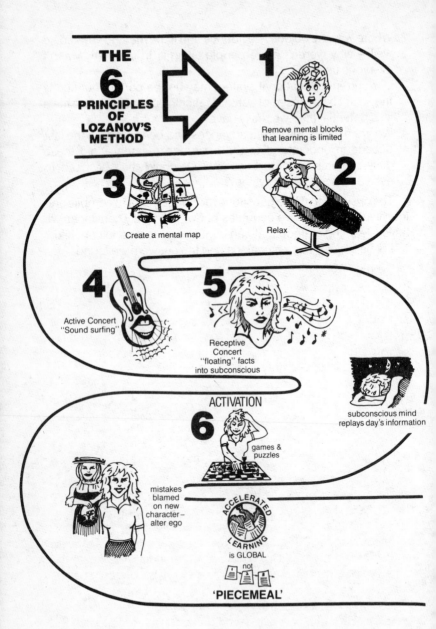

THE **6** PRINCIPLES OF LOZANOV'S METHOD

1 Remove mental blocks that learning is limited

2 Relax

3 Create a mental map

4 Active Concert "Sound surfing"

5 Receptive Concert "floating" facts into subconscious

subconscious mind replays day's information

ACTIVATION

6 games & puzzles

mistakes blamed on new character – alter ego

ACCELERATED LEARNING is GLOBAL not 'PIECEMEAL'

WHAT IS THE ROLE OF THE MUSIC?

"Music, together with colour, forms the therapy of the future".
Dr. Bernard Jensen.

"Music is the mediator between the life of the senses and the life of the spirit".

Beethoven.

Accelerated Learning is undeniably a breakthrough and one of the elements that most characterises its novelty is the use of music. Yet in many ways this part of the technique was already known to the Ancients. In B.C. Athens, audiences would attend a festival in the Panathenes once every four years. A presenter would chant the entire Iliad to the heartbeat rhythm of a softly playing lyre. From memory. Records show that many of the audience could remember large passages afterwards.

Plato and Aristotle discuss the role of music in "harmonising the soul and body" Plato went further. "The character of a nation's music cannot be altered without changing the customs and institutions of the State".

Confucius echoed the thought:-

"The superior man tries to promote music as a means to the perfection of human culture. When such music prevails, and people's minds are led towards ideals and aspirations, we may see the appearance of a great nation".

John Milton specifically discussed the use of music to relax and dispel fatigue in 'Of Education'. The contemporary monasteries regularly used background music to their priests' studies - the same priests who were able to memorise whole books on religious themes.

The effect of music is not confined to philosophers and poets. There can be no human being who has not been touched by the sheer beauty of a ballet movement, or an evocative piece of music. There is no faster way to create or change moods.

The Shamans of Central Russia and the mystics of India use music to induce a planned state of mind and to control pain. In Tibet, Africa and Morocco music is believed to have a magical quality. Bach wrote the Goldberg Variations specifically to induce sleep for the Russian envoy, Count Kayserling.

Science is now corroborating age old intuition. We know that music using certain types of rhythm, does bring about a state of relaxed alertness and physical calm. It is the predominantly alpha brain wave pattern that psychological researchers find is often associated with meditation. Music can do in minutes what weeks of meditative practice strive towards.

Pythagoras believed that musical rhythm could harmonise mental rhythm. He discovered the mathematical proportion of harmonic ratios and intervals and evolved the philosophy of "the music of the spheres". The musical scale, he believed, was related to the movement, and position, of the planets. It is a nice coincidence that we are again discussing the music of the spheres, although those spheres are now the left and right spheres of the brain.

Rhythm

Rhythm is at the heart of the Universe and the Natural world. The ordered rhythm of the stars and planets. The direct influence of the moon. The rhythms of the seasons. These we acknowledge.

The human being is also governed by rhythm. We all have a precise daily rhythm, our circadian cycle. Our hormones rise and fall in ordered sequence.

That music and rhythm have a direct effect on all living things has been dramatically demonstrated in a series of experiments on plants. Experiments that seem, at first sight, bizarre. They started with tests conducted by Dr. Singh, Head of Botany at the Annamalai University in India. Stimulated by accounts in ancient Tamil literature of peasants using music to stimulate the growth of crops, Dr. Singh played recorded 'lute-like' music to balsam plants. An identically matched group of plants, receiving identical amounts of water, but no music, acted as a control. Within a month the experimentally 'serenaded' plants had 72% more leaves and grew 20% taller.

Further tests sufficiently convinced him to begin a large scale experiment using loudspeakers broadcasting to paddy fields! The resulting harvests were 25% - 60% higher than the regional average.

As these apparently 'freaky' experiments gained publicity, researchers in Canada and Kansas began their own controlled experiments. At Ottowa University, Measures and Weinberger managed to duplicate Russian and American research that showed that ultrasonic frequencies had a marked effect on seed germination and growth and even established that different plants reacted best to different frequencies. They suggested in the Canadian Journal of Botany that the accelerated plant growth they had consistently observed was occasioned by the stimulating effect of resonance on the plant cells.

The experiments that are of most interest to us, however, were conducted by a Mrs Rettallack of Denver. Despite the open ridicule of fellow students at the University, she tested the comparative effect of rock music versus classical music on vegetable plants, petunias, zinnias and marigolds.

The plants in the room receiving rock music either grew abnormally tall, with very small leaves, or remained stunted. In *every* case the plants leaned away from the source of the rock music. Within 2 weeks the flowers died. In the identical control room the plants receiving Baroque compositions, together with the music of Haydn, Brahms and Beethoven, flourished. They outgrew control plants and leaned towards the source of the sound. When she tested Bach and selected classical Indian music, played on the sitar by Ravi Shankar, the plants leaned an unprecedented 60% degrees *towards* the music, and the nearest ones literally grew to wrap themselves around the speakers.

There is no question about the genuineness of either the experiments or the results and it provides interesting circumstantial evidence for the beneficial effect of Baroque and Classical music on simple living organisms.

But how does it happen?

No one knows for sure., We do know, however, that the

Baroque composers were heirs to the belief that there was a sacred geometry about the universe. Nature and the human body was subject to a set of exact ratios and proportions. If these "Golden Means" were reproduced in art, architecture and music, the resulting creations would resonate with a life enhancing force.

We certainly know that one tuning fork, when struck, will cause every other tuning fork in auditory range, to vibrate at the same frequency 'in sympathy'.

As we delve into the micro world of the constituents of the atom, we find that all matter is in a state of vibration. Atoms are harmonic oscillators in which the nuclei are the oscillators themselves and the electrons in their orbits, are the resonators, producing reverberations of the periodic harmonic motions of the nucleii. Individual atoms and molecules have characteristic vibrations. According to physicist Dr. Donald Hatch - "we are finding that the universe is composed not of matter, but of music".

Through the work of Dr. Hans Jenny we can now actually *see* the wave patterns created by musical notes and their effect on varying kinds of matter.

Dr. Jenny's start point was the work of the eighteenth century German Physicist, Ernest Chladni, who scattered sand on steel discs and observed the changing patterns, produced when various notes were played on a violin. The patterns were created because only certain areas of the disc resonated to the notes, causing the sand to be shifted to the areas that were inert. The Chladni figures are works of art.

Dr. Jenny went much further. Working with liquids, metal filings and powders, he discovered that as pitch ascended the musical scale, the harmonic patterns on the disc also changed but not just to the previous mathematically ordered geometric shapes. The new patterns were organic and mimicked, for example, the hexagonal cells of honeycombs and the vanishing spiral of the primitive nautilus shell.

Stephen Halpern has composed some beautiful music for the *specific* intention of creating physical and mental health through sound. He writes in his book, 'Tuning the Human Instrument' that, *"the forms of snow crystals, the mandala faces of the flowers, actually resonate to the harmony of nature. Crystals, plants and human beings can be seen as music which has taken on form."*

Dr. Hans Jenny working with a 'tonoscope' that transforms sounds uttered into a microphone into their visual representation on a video screen, recorded the sound of Hindi sacred syllable 'OHM'. - the world's most common mantra.

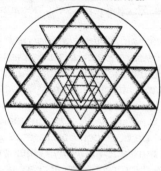

It produced a perfect circle which was filled with concentric triangles and squares. Not only are these symbols found in many of the world's religions but they coincide with the frequency pattern of diminishing harmonics.

Using the same tonoscope, the final chord of Handel's Messiah forms a perfect 5 point star.

We use the phrase that something 'strikes a chord in me'. In London Dr. Manners has actually recorded with a highly sensitive microphone the sound of a human muscle.

The resonance rings true.

Different Music Strikes Different Chords

There is no question that different music has different effects.

Playing Mozart, according to French researcher, Mme. Belanger *"co-ordinates breathing, cardio-vascular rhythm and brain wave rhythm and leads to positive effects on health. It acts on the unconscious, stimulating receptivity and perception."*

In a now famous experiment, subjects were asked to extend their right arm horizontally. Their resistance to downward pressure was measured. The students then relaxed and the experiment was repeated after half an hour but this time rock music (Led Zeppelin) was played. The resistance of every single student was measurably weakened! Classical musical was tested but found to have either a neutral or strengthening effect. You can try it yourself.

Anyone still sceptical about the physical property of music should talk to a professional rock musician. The reason rock, which uses a lot of loud and heavy base guitar, is thought to be sexual, is because it vibrates at a specific frequency which literally vibrates in our loins. Rock seems sexy because it is, physically, sexual.

Mendelssohn once said, *"Music cannot be expressed in words, not because it is vague but because it is more precise than words."*

If a single note during the Jenny experiments can have such a beautiful (and dramatic) effect, it is hardly surprising that a musical piece that is specifically constructed to be harmonious should have a physically harmonious effect on our minds and bodies.

It appears that the Baroque composers, attempting to create an ideal mathematical form and harmony in their music, managed to produce exactly the right frequency and sound to harmonise the functioning of the brain and produce a state of calm, relaxed alertness. This is why so much emphasis, in the development of Lozanov's technique has been placed on Baroque music - largely composed in the period 1700-1750.

Baroque and classical composers tended to employ a constant theme, and they aimed for symmetry or pattern throughout their work. The main key was established clearly at the beginning of the composition. The first and last movements would be in the tonic key and the slow movement was in a key with a very close relationship to tonic.

It was a primary aim of Baroque composers to use music to create a specific unifying mood and to liberate the mind from earthly concerns. Baroque thereby shares a common aim with certain Indian works, which were also written to create a specifically meditative state.

Baroque music is also characterised by contrasts; contrasts between instruments, bright versus dark sounds.

The contrasts continue between movements - fast/slow/fast; contrasts between the upper (treble) melody and lower, deeper (bass) accompaniment. Nevertheless the overall effect of the contrasts was to produce a single harmonious and unified effect.

The violin, considered to be the expressive instrumental counterpoint to the human voice, featured widely in Baroque music, and the continuous base was often the harpsicord plus cello or bassoon.

The rhythm of Baroque music is unusually precise. Generally speaking, the music accompanying our own Accelerated Learning language dialogues, features a clearly recognisable melody in the violin or string section, with a steady bass accompaniment to a specific rhythm of 60 beats per minute. We have favoured composers such as Handel, Vivaldi, Bach, Corelli and Telemann. The effect is to produce a sense of well-being and of relaxed receptivity.

Each concert session is brought to a refreshing and stimulating conclusion with a bright joyful sound - often a flute piece in a major key.

Educational theorist Stephen Cooter monitored his brain wave patterns on an E.C.G. biofeedback machine, while listening to the music recommended for the active concert. He found a 'balanced' and complete brain wave configuration as follows:-

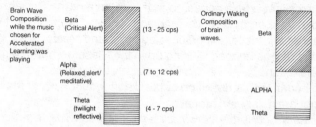

Although the above charts are not exactly to scale, the music had a very measurable effect in increasing the proportion of alpha and theta brainwaves. Studying the effect in detail, Cooter noted, "that largo movements produced a sleepy theta-dominant brain rhythm. When whole classical compositions are used a more balanced and complete brain wave configuration is produced: roughly equal alpha (alert), twilight (relaxed), and beta (critical alert) rhythms are present."

Stephanie Merek, a Lozanov teacher, pointed out that only whole classical compositions are now used in Lozanov classes because they reach and synchronise the whole mind and reproduce the entire *"dynamics of inner life . . . a full 24 hour emotional cycle."*

We cannot help noting in passing, that the characteristic shift in the electro magnetic frequency of brain rhythm which this specific Baroque music produces, is towards 7.5 cycles per second. That is Alpha. 7.5 cycles per second is also the *exact* frequency at which the Ionosphere resonates.

So the Ionosphere, that vacuum layer in the earth's upper atmosphere, which reflects all our radio and T.V. communications, happens to resonate at the precise frequency of the key note of Pythagoras' Music of the Spheres. This 7.5 cps frequency, known as the Schumann Resonance, is also that of the human mind in a meditative state.

Says physicist Robert Beck, contemplating the Schumann Resonance, "The earth itself has a brainwave. There is no longer any question that man is a bio-cosmic resonator."

Let us tune in!

Combining Music, Art and New Perceptions

An excellent article appeared in the Journal of the Society for Accelerative Learning and Teaching (1981), written by Lisa Summer of the Institute for Consciousness and Music, Baltimore Maryland. It was headed 'Tuning up in the Classroom with Music and Relaxation'.

She began with a definition of the differing functions of the left and right brain. It bears repeating.

"Man has a dual brain which allows us to see two, or more,

104

aspects of our environment. The right hemisphere attends to the nonverbal, holistic, spatial and emotional information in the environment. Most of this material is not readily available in our conscious minds. The left hemisphere attends to the verbal, detailed and rational information in the environment. This material is usually available to our conscious mind.

"When the conscious left brain takes control, it results in rigid adherence to the one-sided reality perceived by the left hemisphere. Right hemisphere participation in conscious thinking is actually repressed, and along with it, many of its important unconscious contents.

"Without left and right hemisphere integration, creativity is diminished, if not impossible. In creating, one combines information or ideas in new and unexpected ways. If there is no information or a limited amount of information, then the probability that new combinations can be generated is very limited. When the wealth of right hemisphere impressions are processed with those of the left, the amount and diversity of resources for creating are effectively doubled, hence increasing the capacity for creativity. Despite its importance in both mental health and creativity, the integration of the hemisphere of the brain is not encouraged in our educational system (Galin). Rather, schools tend to reinforce the dominance of the left hemisphere with their emphasis on verbal and deductive subjects. Right hemisphere skills such as music, art, fantasy and even originality, are often considered by school systems to be unessential or counterproductive in the classroom. After many years of learning in such a school system, left hemisphere thinking naturally becomes predominant and the right hemisphere falls to disuse.

"We can avoid handicapping our children by helping them to integrate their two hemispheres. The right hemisphere should be provided with a non-verbal medium through which it can express its contents. Research has shown that music directly stimulates right brain functioning. Therefore it can be used effectively in the classroom to stimulate children to express unconscious feelings and thoughts (Bonny 1973)"

Testing Music and Imagery

In 1982 researchers, B. Stein, C.A. Hardy and H.L. Totten at the University of North Texas conducted a three way test.

They aimed to teach 3 groups of students a list of vocabulary. The students were post-graduates. Each group received a pre-test identical to the post test, and a list of the words to study.

Groups 1 heard the list of words with a background of Handel's Water Music and were asked to visualise the words.

Group 2 heard the same list, but with music only.

Group 3 only read the word list.

Groups 1 and 2 had a significantly improved performance over Group 3 and Group 1 had a very significant advantage over the other two groups when tested a week later.

The researchers concluded that this was consistent with the fact that 'multi-channels' of input stimulate more than one part of the Triune brain vertically (Mclean), and also stimulated a left/right brain connection horizontally (Sperry and Bradshaw & Nettleton).

One Picture is worth 1000 words

The literature research we had conducted on the role of music in Accelerated Learning, was underlined by a clinching piece of evidence from a study done at London University.

Using special brain scan machines that measured the electrical activity of the brain, we were able to actually *observe* the effect of music on the two brains.

The brain scans opposite show:-

a) The brain at rest.

b) A subject merely listening to conversation. His left brain only is activated. (The speech centre was 'switched' on.)

c) A subject just listening to music. You can see clearly that it is the right brain only that is engaged in activity and the language centre on the left has faded.

d) A subject listening to synchronised words and music (e.g. an Accelerated Learning Active Concert). The synchronised activity of left and right brains is clear for all to see.

Since the above electrical brain scanning technique was evolved, a new technique called TOMOGRAPHY has been developed by Professor Michael Phelps of the University of California at Los Angeles. It uses radioactive chemicals to mark out the brain's active areas and a scanner to detect the chemical.

Tomography has not only confirmed the left brain's dominance in processing verbal information and the right brain's dominance in music but has added the interesting fact that the primary visual recognition centre is at the back of the brain. The more complex the scene being viewed, the more this recognition centre is activated.

When words, music and pictures are all synchronised, the area of the visual recognition centre being activated extends right across the back of the head and appears to link up the two halves of the brain.

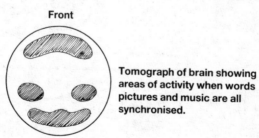

Front

Tomograph of brain showing areas of activity when words pictures and music are all synchronised.

In short, the literature, the University research into Accelerated Learning, and the brain scan experiments, have all convinced us of the effectiveness of the Baroque 'Concerts' in creating an ideal mental state for not only learning but creativity.

MUSIC CREATES & CHANGES MOODS

PYTHAGORAS

RHYTHM

In Russia & India controls pain

"the music of the spheres"

is at the heart of the universe & the natural world

MUSIC & RHYTHM affects all living things

Dr. Singh – India – played music to balsam plants

THE HUMAN BEING is also governed by RHYTHM

the circadian circle

hormone sequence

SINGH BROADCAST MUSIC TO PADDY-FIELDS

The serenaded plant grew 72% more leaves & 20% taller

25 — 60% higher yields

MRS. RETALLAK OF DENVER tested music on vegetables & flowers

BACH & CLASSICAL INDIAN MUSIC

ROCK & ROLL

CLASSICAL

18th century-CHLADNI scattered sand on steel discs formed perfect patterns

plants

snowflakes

TUNING THE HUMAN INSTRUMENT by Stephen Halpern

human beings

can all be seen as music which has taken on form

TONOSCOPE – transform sounds into their visual repres-entation

'OHM' – the world's most common mantra

Mozart music co-ordinates breathing, cardio-vascular rhythm & brain-wave rhythm & leads to better health

LED ZEPLIN
LED ZEPLIN
LED ZEPLIN

Music can weaken or strengthen

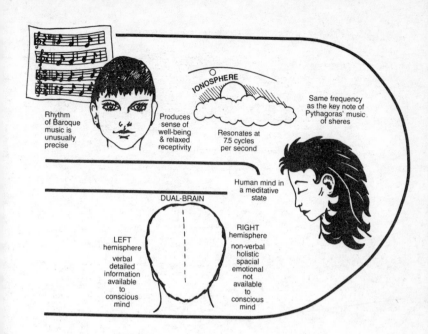

Rhythm of Baroque music is unusually precise

Produces sense of well-being & relaxed receptivity

IONOSPHERE

Resonates at 7.5 cycles per second

Same frequency as the key note of Pythagoras' music of sheres

Human mind in a meditative state

DUAL-BRAIN

LEFT hemisphere

verbal detailed information available to conscious mind

RIGHT hemisphere

non-verbal holistic spacial emotional not available to conscious mind

THE EVIDENCE

When we started to probe, we found that Accelerated Learning is a well researched form of learning. Conventional teaching has been in use for so long that no one thinks to measure it! Accelerated Learning is so fundamentally different that it simply had to be measured and validated to the statistical satisfaction of its originators, its users, and its sceptics.

The evidence falls in two main groups. That conducted by Lozanov in Sophia and the tests and measurements conducted in Europe and the U.S.A. We outline below just a few of the dozens of projects that we surveyed. Before presenting this information, it is important to remember the distinction between learning defined as recognition and learning defined as unprompted recall. The word "learned", is unfortunately not a very precise one. There are standard linguistic tests and where they were used in the tests, we have said so. We are however more impressed with comparative tests i.e. those that directly measured the effectiveness of Accelerated Learning against conventional learning. Results that show that an Accelerated Learning course worked 3 times better than a conventional course, are likely to be more valid than tests which show that (say) 900 words were learned in a day due to the difficulty of evaluating learning on a scale that is universally accepted.

Sophia

In 1967 at Sophia University 416 students were set to learn 1,600 words of French in 31 school days (spending 45 minutes per day). Correct recall means they correctly remembered the meaning of each word when it was given and could use it correctly in a sentence.

> 12% learnt with between 50% and 85% correct recall
> 88% achieved over 86% correct recall

The average correct recall of memorised words was 93%

The achievement is equivalent to acquiring a useable vocabulary of over 1,400 words in one month. To put that in context, it has been calculated that the average reader of a popular tabloid can comprehend a week's issue on a vocabulary of under 1,200 words.

Another way of expressing the results, is that the average student learnt 61 words per 45 minute lesson, within a normal school curriculum. Berlitz, the world's largest teacher of foreign languages, have quoted an average of 200 words after 30 hours - 7 per hour average.

Importantly, the survey revealed that sex, age and education were not relevant to results. There was a minor trend for women to out-perform men and for the under 40's to learn slightly faster, but it should be emphasised that the speed of progress of the over 40's was only 3% less than the under 40's.

Significantly educational background played no part in the effectiveness of the Accelerated Learning techniques.

Of the 416 students under study, 120 had a secondary school as opposed to a higher education background. Their percentage of correctly memorised words was 92.6% as opposed to 93.3% for the University students. The difference of course is statistically insignificant.

But Does It Last?

One of the basic principles of our Calvinistic society is that effort = excellence. Nothing easy is supposed to be worthwhile. "Easy come" is supposed to lead to "easy go". Surely anything easily learnt, will be quickly forgotten?

Lozanov, however, showed that, far from students forgetting the material they learnt using the Accelerated Learning technique, their supermemory, medically known as hypermnesia, proved to have super staying power (hyper durability!).

Short term checks showed a decline from the mid 90% accuracy to 88% average. When a proportion of the same students were given follow up tests, these were the results:-

Original correct recall	93%
After 6 months	88%

After 9 months	85%
After 12 months	67% (79%)

The figure in brackets shows the correct recall percentage for a sub-group who were allowed to make just one revision of the material.

Using the Ebbinghaus curve of forgetting, we could expect that the percentage of correctly remembered material using conventional learning would have declined to about 20% after a year - and this checks very well with later tests where a control was used, i.e. a group of students who were taught this same syllabus but with conventional teaching techniques.

In contrast the Lozanov taught language registered a 67% correct recall after a year - 3 times as effective. Source: "Outlines of Suggestopaedia". Published by: Gordon & Breach N.Y.

The 'Hindi Test' - Hypermnesia proves to have a cumulative effect.

A frequent comment from students using Lozanov's Accelerated Learning was "my general memory seems to have improved".

This led Dr. Lozanov to the Hindi test. 141 students, who were about to embark on a Accelerated Learning course, were given 100 words of Hindi to learn. They leant the words using their normal methods, before embarking on their Accelerated Learning French Language course. They scored an average 33.9% correct.

They then were put through their French course for a month.

At the end of the month they were given 100 more words of Hindi to learn, in the same time and again under normal, non-Accelerated Learning conditions. This time their correct recall was 50.2%. The effect of one Accelerated Learning Course appeared to show a near 50% improvement in their general ability to memorise.

This type of experiment was repeated with mathematical problems, and again there was a significant improvement in overall learning ability.

These tests have real significance. We believe, supported by a wealth of practical and qualititive experience, that we can look to

113

a time when a significant positive shift in overall learning ability and I.Q. is possible, because the methods used in Accelerated Learning result in general mental training.

What happens to the brain during an Accelerated Learning Concert?

Lozanov measured the effectiveness of each part of the Accelerated Learning course and pinpointed the 'concert' stage - where the language session has a background of classical music - as the single most effective part of the course.

He set up measurements of the student's brain waves while they experienced Accelerated Learning, using a E.E.G. (electro-encephlograph) machine, which records brain wave patterns.

The most noticeable conclusion was that during the concert sessions, the proportion of the students Alpha brain wave output increased - from 30% to 40% and Beta waves dropped from 55% to 47%.

A rise in Alpha brain waves is associated with relaxation and meditation. So the part which is designed to produce maximum memory coincided exactly with the point of maximum relaxation. This would also explain why the students almost unanimously expressed pleasure that they felt so refreshed after the Accelerated Learning sessions.

Accelerated Learning and Sleep Patterns

It is well established that our night's sleep is characterised by several stages. The stage called paradoxical sleep or 'Rapid Eye Movement' sleep, normally accounts for 20-25% of a night's sleep in adults. This type of sleep occurs about four times a night and is the time when we dream and in which Rapid Eye Movement (REM) occur. It is also known, therefore, as REM sleep. As we have seen, many psychologists believe that we review and process the information of the day during REM sleep.

Lozanov theorised that students should experience an increase in REM sleep after an Accelerated Learning session, because they had vastly more information to process than usual.

Accordingly, a group of students were connected to E.E.G. machines to measure their brain wave patterns during REM sleep and its duration. It was found that the duration of Rapid or Paradoxical sleep increased by 50%.

Moscow

The V.I. Lenin Institute in Moscow is perhaps Russia's most prestigious foreign language academy. It has embraced the Lozanov system after a series of carefully controlled tests conducted and reported by N.L. Smirnova in 1973.

The test was a four way design.

      Group 1 learnt English using conventional teaching
      Group 2 learnt English using Accelerated Learning
      Group 3 learnt French using conventional teaching
      Group 4 learnt French using Accelerated Learning

There were 25 students in each group. The results were:-

	English		French	
Period of teaching	Vocabulary of Control (conventional Teaching)	Vocabulary of Acc. Group	Vocabulary of Control (conventional Teaching)	Vocabulary O Acc. Learning Group
1st month (21 days)	570	1,600	420	1,740
2nd month (18 days)	420	950	407	790
TOTAL:	990	2,550	827	2,530

1. The highlights of the test, reported in a very understated tone by Dr. Smirnova, were

1. Students using Accelerated Learning learnt the basis of a new language in a month.
2. The students did not show signs of fatigue in spite of the large amount of material. They reported a 'Sense of satisfaction' and most of them felt that 'the barrier of shyness had been removed'. Many also reported better sleeping and a disappearance of headaches and depression.
3. The basis of the evaluation was words accurately remembered according to standard language test procedures.

4. The grammar vocabulary and colloquial fluency of the Accelerated Learning group was very substantially better - the length of their sentences was greater and their syntax was more complicated. Indeed their overall performance was three times better at least - but their spelling was only equal to the control groups - an inevitable result of the concentration on the oral side of language learning.

The report went on to say that the Accelerated Learning groups had a 'considerable advantage in understanding an unfamiliar text'.

These conclusions are not unexpected, because they are exactly true of the way we naturally learn our own language as children.

Budapest

A test on 20 students was carried out by M. Rabcsak in 1979 in Budapest. 12 students were assigned to learn German and 8 English. It is worth quoting verbatim the first paragraph of the conclusions from the official report:-

"When they compared the conventional teaching of a foreign language with Accelerated Learning, the committee noticed a surprising fact. After four years of instruction, the best secondary school students would assimilate from 2,000 to 3,000 words. They would typically make active use of about 1,000 words, with a rather tardy readiness to engage in conversation. The remaining two thirds of what has been learnt forms a passive stock of words, a large part of which are quickly forgotten. In the first Accelerated Learning course the students mastered nearly 2,000 words in 23 days. Of these words they actively employ between 1,200-1,500 words using them readily in conversation.

"Forty five days after the completion of the course, a delayed check was carried out. In the case of a few people, the results obtained from the check showed a one or two percent drop. The majority of students, however, showed an increase of two or three and a half percent. This is entirely different from the effect of conventional teaching.

"One of the students attended the German language course in the morning and the English language course in the afternoon. This

parallel teaching yielded excellent results - better than the other students! Though one cannot of course be definitive on the basis of a sample of one, the examiners concluded that the 'state of enhanced receptiveness increased the effectiveness of the next lesson'."

The Western Evidence

As information on Accelerated Learning began to disseminate during the late 1970's and early 1980's, educationists in the U.S.A., excited at the claim of a 3, 5 even 7 times speed up in learning rates, decided to put the Accelerated Learning techniques to the test. Centres of study began to spring up almost organically.

Iowa State University

An influential early area was Iowa State Univeristy, home of Clincial Psychologist Dr. Don Schuster, Professor of Psychology at the University. At the beginning his research inevitably involved trial and error. He had no idea whether any one element was the key or, as we now know, whether it was a subtle and harmonious combination of many elements that produces Accelerated Learning.

The first experiments, therefore, were focused on relaxation. Students were taught yoga-like relaxation, and then lessons were simply accompanied by classical background music using a normal textbook. The subject was Spanish. The test worked and Schuster founded the previously noted SALT - Society for Accelerated Learning and Teaching.

FOOTNOTE

SALT is the Acronym for "Society for Accelerative Learning and Teaching". It was founded by Professor Dr. Schuster of IOWA State University. It is an association of University personnel engaged in psychological and educational research, together with professional teachers. Members are actively involved in introducing Accelerated Learning into school and college systems. SALT has members in 20 countries and the organisation holds an annual conference each year. The 1984 and 9th Annual Conference was held in Houston U.S.A., and attended by hundreds of professionals. The 10th Conference was held in Washington in May 1985.

In May 1984 a European SALT conference was held in Stockholm, to review European progress. Another European conference was held in London in May 1985, under the auspices of SEAL.

Schuster recorded a three-fold increase in learning speed during this first test and this prompted a State grant for further development. He then began to integrate all the elements of the Accelerated Learning techniques to produce a successful University language teaching course.

The Iowa State results encouraged Des Moines teacher, Charles Gritton, to experiment with teaching maths using the same technique. Two Georgia teachers Allyn Pritchard and Jean Taylor further applied Accelerated Learning to elementary school children with retarded reading problems. Pupils were able to catch up a one year gap in reading ability in 14 weeks.

As word spread, many more projects were commenced.

U.S. Navy Tests

Dr. E. Peterson of Iowa State University used Accelerated Learning methods to instruct U.S. Navy recruits, and was able to divide the year's intake up into two groups. One half was taught with Accelerated Learning techniques, one half conventionally. As with all such experiments, he found that the Accelerated Learning group learnt at least 2-3 times faster. What makes his experiment worth special note, however, was the fact that he also adminstered a questionnaire to the Accelerated Learning students to uncover some of their attitudes towards the technique after the course was completed.

He noted in a preamble that *'the Lozanov class were full of sparkle and desire to learn. That made teaching rewarding and enjoyable. Absenteeism was very, very low. I shall use the technique full-time from now on'.*

Results of the questionnaire were:-

Liked the Lozanov method:- yes 92% no 4% no opinion 4%

Were you interested in the subject:- very 70% quite 30%

The Paradise Unified School Project

In 1982 School Psychologist Roy Applegate, of the quaintly named town of Paradise, (California)* applied for a U.S. Government Research Grant to apply Accelerated Learning techniques to the teaching of school children of grades 2-6, ages 6 to 10.

The full report is reprinted as Appendix A at the end of the book.

It is especially significant, however, because it is an objective report from an independent Government financed investigation unit. The test involved 850 students and 33 teachers over a two year period.

The results showed:-

*a dramatic increase in student learning rates in reading, maths, spelling and writing'.

* 'a significant improvement in classroom behaviour'.

* 'students gained nearly twice as much in Accelerated Learning classes as in control classes (ie. taught conventionally)'

* 'Project teachers continued (after two years of using the method) to demonstrate high levels of confidence and class room control'

The fact that this large scale study showed a two times speed up in learning rates, whereas the tests on adults averagely show at least a three times speed up, is to be expected. In the Paradise School study the ages were 6-10 which is anyway a period of fast learning.

Press Comment

There have now been hundreds of articles in the American Press giving details of the effectiveness of Accelerated Learning in the class room.

Harpers Bazaar in its September 1980 edition ran a complete article on Accelerated Learning under the headline "High Speed Learning - Speak another Language in Days".

The article perceptively identified a key aspect to Accelerated Learning - the fact that the human mind really is capable of undreamed feats when learning blocks have been removed. The Accelerated Learning programme, they reported 'are geared to help dissolve fear, self blame and negative suggestions about limited abilities. In its place they create positive expectations of high rates of success'.

FOOTNOTE

Paradise, whilst actually a very attractive town on the Nevada Border is named after the casino rather than the topography. The towns name is actually a corruption of the phrase "pair of dice"!

The most spectacular case they reported was of a class who were introduced to French one morning. After a day's continuous instruction using Accelerated Learning they were given a test. The class average correct recall was 97%. They had apparently learned 970 words of French in a day!

Now whilst the basis measurement (not quoted in the article) must have been recognition of the English meaning of each given French word, there was one point of significance in the test. The students were never told the scope of the experiment at the outset. The researchers were sure (no doubt with justification!) that the instinctive reaction of the class would have been that to learn a 900 words in a day *'was impossible'*. The experiment quite clearly showed that *'impossible'* is only in the mind.

Lozanov Learning Institute

The Lozanov Learning Institute in Silver Springs, Maryland, which was the organisation specifically licensed by Dr. Lozanov himself, has taught students from many of Americas top corporations.

They include UNESCO officials, ARAMCO, A.T. & T., Bell Telephones, Touche Ross, Saudi Arabian Airlines, Delta Airlines, General Motors, Hilton Hotels, The Department of Commerce, the Defence Department and State Department of the U.S. Government, Shell Oil and literally hundreds of major organisations.

Public funds have now been granted to install Accelerated Learning techniques in locations of both higher learning and primary learning and the Institute now has contracts to install the Lozanov method in the public school system in Chicago, in Bristol, Virginia and in Detroit.

Within the last two years (1983) the U.S. Foreign Service Institute has begun using the Accelerated Learning techniques to teach certain foreign languages and we were told that its direct Russian equivalent in Moscow has done likewise.

Learning to Learn

At least five organisations in North America now teach "Learn to Learn" courses based on principles of the Accelerated Learning.

Charles Schmid of the LIND Institute, San Francisco, the Paradise School Project (already mentioned and originally trained by Charles Schmid,) the Barzakov Institute, and independent consultants Win Wenger of Project Renaissance, Gaithersburg and Paul Hollander, an Educational Planning Consultant of Willowdale, Ontario, Canada. The first three are successful exponents of the basic Lozanov methods, the last two have been working on learning methods that are compatible with Lozanov's principles and which indeed provide important improvements on them.

Charles Schmid now travels extensively to conduct teacher training courses in many countries. In the last year he has conducted training courses at Stellenbosch University, Cape Town, Houston University, Louisiana State University and has now trained scores of Finnish teachers in Accelerated Learning.

Charles Schmid is a true Polymath. He has University degrees in Music, Psychology, French and German. He taught languages for many years at New York University and at the University in Austin, Texas. In 1975 he trained directly with Dr. Lozanov in Sophia and set up his Institute in San Francisco shortly afterwards.

Schmid has refined and extended Lozanov's original methods, and his teacher training courses are now so successful, that we have outlined some of his thinking in a later chapter.

At the Barzakov Educational Institute, in San Francisco, directors Ivan Barzakov and Pamela Rand run a continuous series of workshop courses. According to Barzakov - originally a leading instructor with Lozanov in Sophia - the workshop *'engages participants with art, classical music, theatre, dance and games together with traditional instructional materials, to achieve whole brain learning'*.

Everything in the environment, colours, sounds, textures, rhythms, shapes, even the appearance of the text, are significant in the learning process.

'We orchestrate all these stimulating elements' says Bazarkov, *'and emotional, physical and mental energies are blended to elicit the brain's full capabilities.*

'The mind does not perceive just detailed bits and pieces, but is constantly weaving a large pattern from our experiences. If you

feed it with multi-impressions, that are harmonised and orchestrated to achieve a specific objective, there's practically nothing it cannot learn'.

Ivan Barzakov is unquestionably a sensitive teacher (he wanted to be a musical conductor) and he is clear from his students' reactions that the Lozanov-derived techniques he uses are not just effective in accelerating learning, but in liberating more creative potential than most ever imagine is inside them.

In his classes he invokes his students to be open minded. *'Often you will not, cannot, sense how much you are learning'* he says. *'Trust your intrinsic ability and you'll be amazed at how fast your memory and creativity develops. But do give it time'.* He quotes Epictetus - *'No great thing is created suddenly, anymore than is a bunch of grapes or a fig. If you tell me that you desire a fig, I answer you that there must be time. Let it first bloom, then become a fruit, then ripen'.*

Having seen Ivan orchestrating a class and teaching in a captivating melodious tone of voice, I can confirm he does indeed make his students *'bloom'.* He emphasises self instruction and self development because, as he says, *'No one can teach you but yourself'.*

European Experience

In the last two to three years Accelerated Learning projects have begun in many European locations.

Teachers in the *Finnish* primary school system have adopted the technique on a country wide basis.

In *Denmark,* Vibeka Cristofoli is working with Amnesty International to teach Danish to Polish, Vietnamese and South American refugees and runs teachers training courses at the Institute of Educational Development in Copenhagen. She also finds the Accelerated Learning relaxation technique beneficial in rehabilitating stroke victims.

Uppsala University, *Sweden,* is applying Accelerated Learning techniques to many of their degree courses.

A Lozanov Institue has opened up in *Germany* and *Lichtenstein* headed by professional teacher Tony Stockwell.

In *Paris* there is the Lycee Voltaire School run by Jean Curreau, and at Ecole Francaise de Suggestopedie, Rue Henri Barbusse, ex-Sorbonne lecturer Fanny Safaris is offering an Accelerated Learning Course teaching English.

Several articles have appeared in the French newspapers on Fanny Safaris' courses. Journalist Judith Monthie writes.

'Students settled back in their lounge chairs, with pillows under their heads and blankets over their knees, listening to a concert by Bach or Mozart while their teacher reads the text to be used for the next two to three days. Her voice is controlled just like another musical instrument to fit the rhythm, pauses and moods of the music. It's an almost sublime moment in language learning: everyday French read as a beautiful work of art! The effect is stunning. All the sessions have this mark of pleasure, of warm ambiance, of gaiety, of ease of communications. Mistakes don't seem important, what counts is the desire to understand and to be understood. Everything possible is done to enhance the student's self-image.

'Looking back on the intellectually cold, mechanically bound 60's and 70's when the teacher was a one-man show with audio visual equipment, tape recorder, slide projector and language laboratory, the giver of all knowledge, the centre of attention in a classroom, the caster of pearls, we've come full circle to the idea that the student is the raison d'etre of a classroom and not the teacher. The student had graduated to a full human being status. Bravo!'

When we talked to Fanny Safaris she told us that her Accelerated Learning classes were showing a three times speed up in learning and that this had been confirmed, using recognised linguistic tests by Shell Oil and the Nationalized Thompson Electronics Company.

She identified the key elements in the method as being:-

(a) A direct channel to both the subconscious and logical mind simultaneously.

(b) A relaxed and pleasant atmosphere. The joy of learning in a practical form.

(c) The presentation of a large amount of material quite quickly thereby implying an expectation of success.

(d) The realisation that you do not have to learn every word exactly to progress to the next lesson. To learn 300 words a day in a relaxed mood and with 80% recall (240 correct) is undeniably a superior achievement to learning 50 words a day at 100% accuracy with grim determination.

(e) The regaining of a child-like capacity to play *'Laughter'* quotes Fanny, *'Lubricates learning'*.

England

In Britain the two principal exponents of Accelerated Learning are the School of English Studies (S.E.S. at Folkestone, Kent) and the Western Language Centre at Kemble, Gloucestershire. Both are approved by the Department of Education. The Principal of the School of English Studies (S.E.S.) is Peter O'Connell. We asked him to comment not so much on the technique of Accelerated Learning but its effects on his students. His answer was revealing.

'Healthy children learn their native tongues with joy and efficiency. As soon as they go to school the shades of the prison house descend. Some pupils are lucky and enjoy some years in Kindergarten and Primary school. Secondary school, however, with its obsessive concern with examination and grades and reports, associates learning in most pupils' minds with pain and boredom and anxiety.

'A thirty-five year old Swiss Banker was celebrating the completion of a six week intensive English Course. He said to me, "I really enjoyed the past six weeks here - and yet I'm sure I've learnt a lot of English".'

'Surely the two go together' I replied, *'If you have enjoyed yourself, you are more likely to have learnt well'*. Yet the proposition was difficult for the Swiss Banker to accept. This professionally successful man sadly confessed that he hadn't derived any pleasure from his school studies and even his University years had been boring. How many successful business and professional people have a similarly sombre memory of their formal education?

In the process of achieving a state of relaxation that makes learning a new language a pleasure, the identity issue is very important. One cannot learn someone else's language unless one can to some extent identify with the native speaker. This means relinquishing, or at least loosening one's grip on one's own national identity. This is a delicate issue, for all of us cling to our identities as to a life-raft. In Folkestone, as I suspect in most language schools, we have partially solved this problem - by use of Christian names.

One day an Italian lady, wife of a banker who had recently completed a four-week course, visited the school. As she came through the door she exclaimed *'What have you done to my husband? Since he came back from Folkestone he's a different man. He was getting so boring. Now he's the life and soul of the party!'*

Conclusion

We have completed a four-year investigative tour that has spanned 3 continents and twelve countries. A list of some of the 40 major University Centres involved is given in Appendix C.

We talked to numerous East European Education Officials, to UNESCO, the U.S. Government funded Centre for Applied Linguistics at Arlington, Virginia. We interviewed Don Schuster of Iowa State University; current SALT President Robert Prall from University of Texas at Houston; IBM Consultant Paul Hollander in Canada; Fanny Safaris from Paris; Ivan Bazarkov of the Optima Learning Institute, San Francisco. Jane Bancroft of Toronto, University of Canada; Luiz Machado of the University of Rio de Janeiro, Brazil; Wil Knibbler of the Katholieke University, Nijmegen, Holland; Christer Landahl of Uppsala University, Sweden; the lozanov Institutes in Washington, Virginia and Vaduz, Lichtenstein, and in England with Peter O'Connell from S.E.S., Folkestone, and Michael Lawlor of the Western Language Centre, Kemble, in Gloucestershire.

They were all of one accord. Accelerated Learning is a teaching method of enormous potential.

Says Peter O'Connell, a normally conservatively spoken man and a leading figure in the teaching of English as a Foreign Language, *'it has the potential to make it possible for the generality of learners to achieve the results reached in our present society only by the small minority of people we call geniuses'.*

Everyone we spoke to acknowledged the seminal role of Dr. Lozanov, but they were equally sure that Accelerated Learning had progressed far beyond the methods of one man. Accelerated Learning is now a movement. A movement to which thousands of professional teachers and educational psychologists are contributing. It is a style of teaching, a style of presentation, that is still evolving and we have been privileged in this book to bring you not only the *state of the art* but the way to incorporate it into your own life.

THE EVIDENCE

A. Research in Sophia-

B. Measurements & Research in USA, Russia & Europe

A. In 1967 416 students set to Learn 1600 French words in 31 lessons in 31 days

1. 93% CORRECT. Average student learnt 61 words per 45 min lesson!

2. The Hindi Test

BEFORE 33.9% CORRECT

ONE MONTH of Accelerated Learning French Course

AFTER 50.2% CORRECT I.E. Accelerated Learning improves general ability to learn

3. ACTIVE CONCERT

EEG MACHINE Rise in Alpha & Decrease in Beta

Information of the day is reviewed & processed during REM

Accelerated Learning sessions increased REM by 50%

B. 1. RUSSIAN EVIDENCE

Smirnova at Lenin Institute

2. HUNGARIAN EVIDENCE

No mental fatigue students

3. AUSTRIAN EVIDENCE

Lester Kaplan Taught employees of Nestlé 50-60 words per hour without stress

conventional teaching 2000 to 3000 words in 4 years

Through Accelerated Learning students mastered nearly 2000 words in 23 days!

4. AMERICAN EVIDENCE

Iowa State University Dr Don Schuster 3 Fold improvement

PARADISE UNIFIED SCHOOL PROJECT

After 2 years — significant improvement in learning rate

6-10 year olds

TELL ME...

1. Does our Educational system really teach us to doubt our true ability?

A central principle of Accelerated Learning is that we must first unshackle ourselves from the belief that we have limited ability.

It seems illogical, or at the very least ironical, that we should subconsciously restrict our own abilities. Yet we do.

Education expert Stephen Cooter writing in the Society for Accelerated Learning and Teaching (S A L T) Journal emphasises that education *used* to be holistic. Subjects were not originally isolated from each other. Music for example was taught in relation to mathematics. He writes:-

'When grammar is connected with literature, neither grammar nor literature are forgotten. When information is given a rich context of connections, it is easily remembered and used. In contrast, when you look at modern presentations of information, you find that you are informed by specialists who know more and more, about less and less. History textbooks are frequently dry inventories of facts. Grammar texts are dry inventories of rules without explanation or life-like connections. When people study isolated items of information, they are attempting to remember things equivalent to nonsense syllables which are rapidly forgotten.'

The point is echoed by teacher trainer Valerie Beeby in a private letter to me. "The assumption that we have limited ability paradoxically stems from the very process by which we progressed from the restrictive thinking of early medieval times.

In those 'dark ages' in Europe, all knowledge was believed to have been discovered already, and to be contained in the books of the 'ancients', written in Latin and held in the monasteries. Either it was not your place to learn things; or if it was, all knowledge was there for the reading. There was little question of finding out anything new. If you wanted to know how bees behaved, you did not study bees, but looked to see what Aristotle said about them.

An active, acquisitive mind, in fact, was a positive disadvantage. You could be burned at the stake! It was no accident that the churchman held tight control of 'all knowledge' in their libraries - and upheld the use of Latin for learned discourse.

Then people began to rebel. Leonardo da Vinci in Renaissance Italy. Francis Bacon in Elizabethan England who died of a chill which he caught after getting out of his coach on Highgate Hill to put a chicken in the snow. (He wanted to see if the cold would preserve it!)

Men like da Vinci and Bacon had started to look at the world around them, and see that there was still a good deal to discover. It was no longer enough to believe something just because it was in a book.

All this produced an enormous increase in knowledge, freed people's minds from the stranglehold of dogma, and gave rise to a host of new and ingenious inventions. It produced, in fact, the modern world.

Unfortunately, it had side effects.

The side effects can be seen simply as three major splits, all forms of over-specialisation. Each split produced, along with the new freedom, a new limitation on people's realisation of their own capacities.

In the first place, there was the split between subject and subject. The famous 'Renaissance Man' had been skilled in a wide range of subjects: music, mathematics and medicine; art and astrology; dancing and divinity. But with the expansion of knowledge, it was no longer believed feasible to know everything about everything.

Enter the specialist, narrowly versed in his own subject and ignorant of others. It has been noted more than once that the canteen is often the most productive department in a research establishment. The canteen is the only place where specialists meet and informally exchange notes, together with personal details not usually considered relevant in formal discussions. The result is often a new angle on their work - and a new discovery or invention.

The second split is the well known one between the 'two cultures', science and the arts. When it was realised, with the development of scientific enquiry, that a hunch, or even a firmly held conviction, could be proved wrong by an experiment, scientists began to put less and less trust in their own gut reactions. The model scientist was a being totally unswayed by passion or human feelings, able to abstract general laws with sublime independence. Personal reactions were for the Arts people, who if they were at all scientific in their methods, had to conceal this under a florid cloak of Bohemianism, just as the scientist had to hide his emotions under his spotless white coat.

The division goes deep, to the extent that many a scientist, thinking abstractly, is unaware that he is consistently having recourse to mental images, rhythms, even bodily sensations, properly thought the domain of the artist.

The poet T S Eliot refers to the split in a famous essay as a *'dissociation of sensibility'*, and points out that to the Elizabethan "Metaphysical" poet, *'a thought was an experience'*. Later, thought and experience parted company; even, for poets, let alone scientists.

Both of these splits are well recognised today, and both often cause us to place severe limitations on our own mental capacities.

The third split came with the invention of ingenious machines for mass production, the industrial revolution. It was the split between the bosses and the assembly line workers.

The emphasis in the schooling of the workers shifted at this time to training these citizens to be efficient 'producers' and 'consumers'. Even the words are dehumanising.

Specialisation, assembly line co-operativeness, and, as a byproduct, restricted-thinking mechanical efficiency, became highly prized attributes. It was natural that educational systems to turn out these ideals would be developed in parallel.

As so many social historians have noted, when a craftsman designed, made (and often sold) the product of his labour, the work carried much more satisfaction. When the work became fragmented and specialised into simple, but highly repetitive tasks, the result was high dissatisfaction, absenteeism and a general impression amongst the work force that they had limited potential.

It cannot be accidental that when the techniques of industrial management - and social engineering - were applied to education, the result was exactly the same. Indeed in 1923 the U.S. National Research Council actually convened a three way conference between representatives of the Government, industry and educators, the purpose of which was *'to standardise measurements of education'* and to *'standardise human beings'*. These were the *exact* words used.

The legacy of this type of thought on school architecture and teaching methods lasted 50 years. We believe that this attitude has contributed to many of the learning blocks. If you are attempting to train people to become efficient and quiescent cogs in society's wheels, you hardly need (or dare) to create much independence of thought or creativity.

The role of the teacher as foreman, overseeing a standardised curriculum, is hardly a far stretched metaphor.

Fortunately, we are now in the middle of the post industrial revolution. The new robotic and electronic technology that will free human beings from the drudgery of repetitious and mind numbing work, can be matched by the new methodology of Accelerated Learning which can in parallel free the mind.

Today's teachers recognise that the classes where there is warmth, a positive atmosphere and general participation, are the classes in which most is learnt and remembered.

Just how severely our expectations of our own abilities have been constricted, is well illustrated by an interesting experiment conducted by Georgi Lozanov. He set out to measure just how many words of a new foreign language it was possible to teach in a day. (The reason why so much work has been done on languages, is that progress in vocabulary is easier to quantify than for most other subjects.)

The test showed that the more the students were taught the more they learnt! After 800 class days - a significant sample - this was the result.

1. When the session (day) was designed to teach 100 new words the rate of correct recognition was 92%
2. When the session was designed to teach 200 new words it was 96.8%

3. When the same sessions were boosted to 1,000 new words *in a day* the correct recognition was 96.1%!

Lozanov's conclusion is fascinating. Accelerated Learning seems to work not by actually increasing the capacity of the human memory, but by overcoming the expectation that memory is limited. In other words it de-suggests the negative expectations of limited ability we have built up throughout our normal learning experiences, and allows our innate natural mental ability to operate more fully. (Remember the hypnotised weight lifter?)

This explanation must be correct, because if we did not have latent ability, the suggestion would only arouse a hope, without the possibility of it's being fulfilled.

At a learning rate where the students could, just, envisage being able to learn using conventional methods, they were tempted to try and use both the conscious and subconscious learning stimuli. When the rate of learning escalated so far above the accepted norm, the students relaxed their apprehension and allowed themselves to be carried along by the techniques.

The clear lesson is relax and let it all happen!

The suggestion that learning is going to be difficult is built up in many subtle ways. The fact that text books visibly start with the ultra simple and get progressively more complex, (the linear approach), reinforces the assumption that complex equals harder. In conventional teaching, simple elements are repeated constantly with the promise that later they will be fitted into the 'big picture'. Yet this is *not* how psychologists have found the brain works. A recent psychology article points out that:-

'*It is well known that there is NO case where the brain functions only with its cortical structure (conscious) or only with the subcortex (subconscious). The functional unity of the cortical-subcortical system is indissoluble.*

'*Teaching practice where the instruction is addressed only to the cortical structure regards the pupil as an emotionless cybernetic machine*'.

Yet that is what most left brain teaching effectively does. Even a good teacher usually regards the teaching process in stages. You normally address the logical cortex first and then later may address the emotional subcortex. Lozanov's breakthrough was to address them simultaneously, since every human operates simultaneously at both the conscious and unconscious levels.

Creating the environment for an Accelerated Learning lesson is a subtle process. A teacher who says *'Today we are going to learn 300 new words. I know you've been conditioned to believe this is impossible, but in fact it's easy and you'll be successful'*, has not a proper understanding of the subtleties of suggestion.

By merely mentioning that 300 words is thought to be impossible, she is alerting her students to be conscious of their learning process. She is effectively saying *'Try, but expect to fail'*. If you have ever gritted your teeth and *tried* to get to sleep you will understand the chances of success. The teacher is also reducing her effectiveness even further by telling her students they are wrong.

Contrast the approach with that of a French teacher using a positive and 'suggestive' approach as quoted by Philip Miele in his book on Accelerated Learning, "Easier Learning in the Natural Way".

'Now let's learn how to check into a hotel in Paris. You already Know now many of the words like "hotel" *and* "baggage" *and* "taxi" "Sa femme" *means his wife, but you probably know that too. Now the first sentence* "Pierre et sa femme arrivent a l'hotel avec leur baggage" *means* "Peter and his wife arrive at the hotel with their baggage".

In an Accelerated Learning class this is the way new material is introduced - easily, gently, in the context of a story that follows the dramatic rules of fiction - with no mention of 300 words. That comes at the end, with a triumphant 'Look, we've learned 300 words today! We're already speaking good French'.

What happened to the mental blocks? They didn't crumble, the teacher worked in harmony with them. Now the students assume they *can* learn 300 words a day - so a negative assumption has been subtly converted into a positive one. There has been no direct antagonistic challenge to the students beliefs. No alerting to the possiblity of failure.

Consumer product advertising, which is rich in suggestive techniques, also knows how to overcome these existing beliefs.

The makers of an instant coffee for example, encountered a

barrier in the public's mind against purchasing their product. Sophisticated projective testing revealed that women believed that using instant coffee was a mark of laziness and lack of family responsibility. Instead of trying to argue against this barrier, a new advertising campaign was evolved to harmonise with it. A new theme was adopted; the busy housewife can better achieve an existing ideal which is to have more time for her children, her husband and her guests, when she uses instant coffee. Sales went up.

The conclusion is that the mind does have barriers, but the way to overcome them is not a full frontal attack. The way is much more a subtle skirting of them. Replacing negative images with positive ones.

2. How to Double your Reading Speed in 20 minutes

One of the best proofs of how we are conditioned to accept one level of ability - yet how easy it is to significantly improve on that ability - is in reading speed.

The basic problem is that, even as adults, we want to "hear" the words in our mind as we read them. We may not literally subvocalise, but it comes to the same thing - because the eye can take in information *much* faster than the ear. So by insisting on "hearing" the words we significantly slow down our reading. We can only "hear" words at approximately 250 words to the minute, we can see them at the rate of 2,000 words a minute or more. If we can learn to read purely on a visual basis we can rapidly multiply our reading speed.

Another problem is that we insist on trying to "see" every word on a line of type. Yet there are an enormous number of redundant words in English. You do not have to see every word to make sense of the material you are reading. If you only read the key words, you would, at minimum, halve the number of words you needed to read - and thereby speed up your reading. You read, not to see every word, but to *comprehend* the sense of the material.

A third problem is that the eye does not take in a line of print in a smooth flowing movement. In fact only the information reaching a specific and small area of the retina called the fovea is seen really sharply. The eye must stop for a fraction of a second to focus a small amount of text on the fovea. So your eye movement is actually made up of a series of skips, thus:-

The dots are where the eye actually stops to register a strong image in the fovea. The words around these points of fixation are in the field of peripheral vision.

Because we read in a series of skips or jerks we are often tempted to back-skip, to check whether we really saw or understood some of the previous words. This back-skipping is common and probably cuts our reading speed down by a third.

You can measurably increase your reading speed in the next twenty minutes by carrying out the two following simple instructions. First, however, read 2 or 3 pages at your normal speed to establish your current reading rate.

1. Start reading each line of print not at the very beginning of the line but three or four words in. Your peripheral vision and the redundant words will ensure you miss no meaning. Similarly, if you finish reading two or three words from the end of the line you will miss nothing either. But you will have reduced the amount of text you need to fixate on and hence increased your reading speed without sacrificing any comprehension.

2. Start to run your finger down the page at an ever increasing speed. It must be *much* faster than you feel it is possible to register anything. Allow your eyes to follow your finger down the page, but look at the middle of the page. Increase the speed until you are spending only 2 or 3 seconds per page! At this rate you will initially perceive everything as a blur. Yet if you persevere you will find a strange thing happen. A few words will begin to stand out on each page - and they will be some of the key words. The words that convey the main argument or story. It is an interesting proof that your brain is in fact subconsciously processing much of the printed page.

This high speed training succeeds in three ways. First it prevents any possiblity of back-skipping. Secondly, it breaks the dependence on "hearing" the words in your head. You are now relying purely on visual reading and this is *essential* to achieve a really fast reading speed.

The third effect is comparable to the effect of driving down the motorway at a sustained high speed. When you do come to slow down to a "normal" speed, you find that what you thought was 40 miles per hour, is in fact 55 miles per hour, or more. You have altered your perception of speed.

In the same way, when you go back to read at your "normal" speed after 20 minutes of very high speed reading - you will find that it is measurably faster than your previous speed.

Florence Schale from Northwest University studied groups of readers and in "The Psychology of Reading Behaviour" reported that most people were capable of reading at 1800-2000 words a minute. That's 10 times the normal speed under the constraint of "auditory" reading.

Having extolled the virtues of one simple speed reading method, you will be amused to learn that most people can achieve the same effect - with the opposite technique!

It is an excellent example of how adaptable we really are - and why it is important for teachers to recognise the fact that students learning styles can be very different.

The "opposite" method works on the basis of what psychologists call "the law of effect". An action will be discontinued if it proves to be unrewarding.

The idea is to *deliberately* practice the very habit you want to eliminate or overcome. Pay full attention to what you have previously done automatically. It is a technique often used to eliminate nail biting, spelling errors, stammering and nervous tics!

In the case of reading you would practice, for five minutes twice a day, to read very slowly. Force yourself to read much more slowly than normal. At the same time imagine yourself developing a reading speed that is even better than your normal one. In the conflict between will and imagination, imagination will always win!

After just two days you will find you are reading much faster because your mind will rebel against a limit it knows you can overcome.

This little digression has served two purposes. It firstly teaches you the secrets of speed reading courses for which regularly sell for many times the cover price of this book! Secondly, it is a microcosm of what Accelerated Learning is about. Given the techniques and given the proof that we really can break out of our self-imposed limits - we can achieve a quantum leap in our capabilities.

3. How does "Peripheral Learning" work?

Dr. Lozanov conducted a series of tests to specifically isolate the effect of what he terms "visual suggestion" in the learning system. One example typifies the complete series.

A group of 500 students were given a list of 10 towns. Five were faintly underlined in colour - but the underlining was almost imperceptible. They were given three minutes to memorise the 10 towns.

They were then given a long list of 180 towns and asked to pick out the 10 on the original list. Having completed this test they were asked if any of the original were underlined and if so in what colour.

The test was repeated at intervals on the 2nd day through to the 60th day and the recall of the original 10 they had consciously tried to learn, followed the expected Ebbinghaus curve of forgetting. The results of the second test, however, was quite the opposite. The subconsciously learned information (the towns with colour underlines) was better remembered as time went by. Whereas recall of the consciously learnt 10 towns declined from 80% to 50%, the correct recall of the underlined words *rose* from 85% to 91%.

In every mental activity there is a central and focussed experience - and several other peripheral ones. (The words peripheral, subconscious and paraconscious are often used interchangeably). The peripheral influences contribute strongly to what is remembered, learned and believed.

It may be the message you are trying to learn, but the medium is vital to your success.

Try to remember a list of facts on a sheet of paper with the minimum of paraconscious influences and its difficult. Try to remember the words of a song and it's comparatively easy. The medium is the key.

Peripheral influences and intuitive insight are the main means through which children learn because their conscious/rational/logical abilities are not yet developed.

What makes a work of art? It certainly isn't just technical proficiency. It is the emotion that directly communicates to and affects the subconscious the limbic system and the right brain.

What makes a great actor? Someone who communciates his part not just with speech, (which is his approach to your conscious left brain), but with his intonation, gesture, body language and authority.

You never approach any learning experience with a truly blank mind. Your previous experiences always influence your attitude.

4. Is the effectiveness of Peripheral Material reduced when you know it exists?

It might be thought that, once you *knew* that you were being taught by a method that used suggestion and an approach to the subconscious, its effect would be reduced.

Not so. At the Lozanov Teaching Institute the results of some 600 students were compared with 40 professional people - psychologists, psychiatrists and full-time teachers, who had spent two weeks analysing the technique. The students achieved 93% recall overall. The professionals achieved 96%.

It is not surprising. Music students study the principle of music, yet of course music affects them as greatly, or even more profoundly, than other people.

5. Surely this sounds a bit like Mind Control?

It is! But not the way the question implies. The problem, as we've just seen, is that we are already brainwashed to accept that we're limited in potential and that can become a self-fulfilling prophesy.

Accelerated Learning, in contrast, promises to remove those learning blocks. It *does* use techniques that appeal directly to the subconscious but these techniques are openly built into the course.

6. So does Accelerated Learning use Subliminal Techniques?

No. There *is* a difference between peripheral communication and subliminal communication, and it's one of degree.

A peripheral communication is one which you could always pull into your consciousness if you choose. For example, in an Accelerated Learning course the English and Foreign texts are printed together. So while you are reading Spanish, the English translation is in your peripheral vision (you see it out of the corner of your eye). This is ethical because you can always bring it into your consciousness at will.

If we were to use a video film however, which flashed the translation for a split second, that would be subliminal. Subliminal literally means "under the threshold" and almost no amount of conscious concentration could detect the technique. This in our view would be unethical because the student is defenceless, therefore it reduces his freedom and constricts his personality.

Peripheral communication in contrast frees his personality because it uses an entirely natural process. We have already seen that we are constantly receiving stimuli from peripheral sources, sources just out of conscious focus, sounds just below conscious range. All the Accelerated Learning technique does is organise and orchestrate these natural phenomena.

Readers who are interested in the technique of subliminal advertising should read the previously mentioned "Subliminal Seduction" by Professor Wilson Key. It is a shocking exposé of advertising techniques exploited by some of the world's best known brand names.

7. Is any one element of the Accelerated Learning Programme of over-riding Importance?

The essence of Accelerated Learning is that learning becomes an enjoyable (literally joy-full) experience, in which tension disappears and in which the whole brain is united. When the conscious and subconscious, the long term and short term memory, the left and right hemispheres of the brain, are all involved and working together, the effect is not just doubled, it is compounded many times.

Just as the effectiveness of Accelerated Learning does not just involve a simple tripling of the speed of learning and/or retention, so the way Accelerated Learning is achieved is not simple. One element without the other is insufficient. A teacher, for example, who merely creates a fun, relaxed environment will not achieve much in the way of improved results. It is only the accumulative effect of the many harmonious, subtle and peripheral stimuli that can achieve the shift from learning at Accelerated Learning.

In an Accelerated Learning course the student's attention is drawn to the meaning of a whole sentence. The pronunciation, vocabulary and grammar are INDIRECTLY absorbed. They become part of the peripheral material. In that way they pass more easily into the subconscious and long term memory. Much of the new taught material is implicilty, not explicilty taught.

In contemplating the working of Accelerated Learning we were reminded of an old joke.

A customs officer, alerted to the possibility of a smuggling attempt, was surprised in the middle of the night by a man with a wheelbarrow filled with straw. Nothing was found. Next night the same man was back again with a straw filled wheelbarrow. Again the straw was painstakingly searched. Again with no result.

This went on for a whole week.

At the end of seven consecutive trips the customs officer was beside himself. He faced the man and said *'All right - you win! I know you're smuggling something in that straw. I'm dying to know what it is - so much so that I promise not to prosecute, if only you'll tell me. So what on earth are you smuggling?'*

The man smiled as he trundled off. *'Wheelbarrows'* he replied.

Our left brain and conscious mind is a bit like the customs officer. It can let an amazing amount of material into our long term subconscious memory, if only we engage in a little harmless diversion!

In fact at Accelerated Learning Language courses we attended, students frequently said that they often surprised themselves by using foreign words they were unaware of knowing. *'It was as if the words had been smuggled into my mind'*said one. *'It seemed like I was remembering words, not learning them'* said another.

8. What is the "Health Bonus" of the Accelerated Learning Course?

Of all the advantages of Accelerated Learning, inevitably attention has focussed most on the speed of learning, because it is measureable, has an immediate payoff and appeals to our action orientated and speed orientated culture. Somewhat less attention is focussed on the sheer joy of learning it brings (though this is an essential ingredient). Even less attention is paid to the fact that so many students receive an important physical and psychological bonus.

Time after time it has been noticed that tension based illnesses disappear during an Accelerated Learning course. Charles Schmid a major U.S. teacher of the Accelerated Learning method says *'It happens so often I don't even notice it anymore'*.

Cecelia Pollock, Professor Emeritus of Lehman College, Long Island has a very enviable success rate with dyslexics. We visited her to discuss her use of Accelerated Learning techniques with young children.

'Our thinking has been permeated with the I.Q. approach' she said, *'We are taught that intelligence is static and for the most part innate. This concept places a ceiling on the learners potential and lowers her own expectations of her learning potential. Therefore we blame our children if poor learning takes place'*. Significantly Cecilia Pollock emphasises that the psychology behind the development of Accelerated Learning denies that intelligence is fixed, but stresses rather that learning *creates* brain capacity.

Dr. Pollock continues, *'This is why my whole philosophy of dealing with teaching disabled children is an optimistic one. They are not stuck with their disabilities. In the Accelerated Learning process we have a real breakthrough for true mental improvement... it's a way of engaging the entire brain at once, the conscious and unconscious at once... all in a positive emotional climate. There is no learning without healing, and no healing without learning'*.

A UNESCO report on a substantial two years study of 2,300 students in school systems exclusively using the Lozanov system, observed that the rate of neurotic disorders and absenteeism was halved - indicating in the most tangible way that school had

142

become more enjoyable and less stressful.

Dr. Cecilia Pollock again, *'Accelerated Learning is a profoundly humanistic system of education for all'. Instead of failure, it offers psychological relaxation and enjoyment. It helps children overcome their school related fears and depressions. Drop outs become remotivated, tensions and anxieties become relaxed and disappear.*

It's destined to usher in a revolution in learning. All the boredom, the drill, the meaningless tests will be swept aside to make way for integrated knowledge, to the tune of music and song, poetry and puppetry, jingles and jokes... Lozanov expects people to be ten feet tall... AND THEY BECOME SO.

9. Are there people who cannot be reached by Accelerated Learning?

Mongolism used to be thought of as irreparable brain damage which caused its victims to remain at a mental age of about three throughout their lives.

When someone said that Mongoloids were geniuses in disguise, the statement sounded bizarre. But a Canadian family took that idea seriously.

They found their child could learn anything that other children could, but simply took longer in the learning process. Their child treasured each thing that he learned, because it was so hard won. Consequently, he pursued the matter further than the average child would. When he was about twenty, the C.B.C. produced a movie on his life history, in which he was the star. The director of the film said he was one of the best actors he had ever worked with.

A similar point was made by Suzuki, the violin teacher, who tried to teach a polio child to play the violin. For the first six months, every time she tried to hold the bow, it flew out of her hand. She went on to become a thoroughly competent violinist.

Anyone can learn, provided enough time is given them to master each essential part of the learning process and providing they believe in their success.

Dr. Pollock's work with dyslexics indicates that the Accelerated Learning method can contribute substantially.

143

10. Do Pupils get an Immediate Sense of Having Learnt?

Sometimes. Sometimes not!

Some people come away from their first Accelerated Learning session absolutely bubbling with enthusiasm. But some feel almost uneasy. The whole technique is so relaxed and stressless, that you feel that you cannot possibly be learning. It is only the next day that you realise you know much more than you thought possible.

After all, the technique is specifically designed to appeal to your subconscious, so you could hardly be expected to be aware of how much you really know.

In addition, if you have spent years convincing yourself that you have a limited ability, you have obviously adapted your behaviour to that belief. When you realise your learning potential is much greater than you thought, you have implicitly taken on a responsibility to develop it. That takes getting used to. Which is one reason why the effect of Accelerated Learning is accumulative, and the more Accelerated courses you take the more your ability grows.

Ironically, it is often the high achievers in our current educational system, who can have initial trouble in adjusting to Accelerated Learning. They have, by definition, succeeded in a primarily left brain system and they probably had to work quite hard to achieve their success. So they have a subconscious vested interest in perpetuating the methods in which they were successful. If suddenly learning becomes fun, relaxed and comparatively easy, it can, initially appear to devalue the effort they originally put in! However, even a few hours exposure to the enjoyment on an Accelerated Learning course soon convinces them.

11. Why should we want to Speed Up Learning?

We should not - unless it can be done without stress. Until now, any speeding up of learning basically involved intensifying existing teaching practice. The same techniques only more so. The results of that intensification make newspaper headlines every few months.

Teenage suicides in Japan; increased rates of child neuroses in Western Europe are all the result of extra strain and pressure put on young minds.

What is urgently needed, therefore, is a new way of teaching which simultaneously improves mental well being. The relaxed process of Accelerated Learning fits that description.

Given that faster learning can now be gentler learning, then we should obviously welcome it. We live in a period when knowledge is growing at an exponential rate. We live in a technocracy where progress involves the mastering of increasing by complex data; learning an ever increasing volume of information. The spoils go to the well informed.

The gift of fast but stress-free learning is literally priceless.

12. How new is Accelerated Learning?

It is new enough for us to have a Patent Pending on the technique! (as described in this book and as executed in the range of cassette courses available).

This is not to say that other researchers have not independently worked on individual elements in the method.

Thus, in addition to Dr. Lozanov, who originated the successful (but inhibitingly named) technique of Suggestology, Colombian researcher, Alfonso Caycedo, Dr. Alfred Tomatis from France and Shinichi Suzuki of Japan, have all shown that learning is facilitated and speeded considerably when a good proportion is subconscious, and when the presentation of learning material is rhythmic.

Tomatis' research has shown that baroque music, and the violin in particular, stimulates the cortex. Suzuki is, of course, famous for his approach to music teaching. He suggests that a short movement or masterpiece is played once everyday to the baby from birth. He also favours baroque composers because of their clear rhythmic structures and uncomplicated harmonies.

After a few months another piece is selected since the first one will have been fully absorbed. The baby now hears two pieces per day. Gradually by this progression the baby grows into a child who is sensitive to music.

Suzuki's pupils usually begin specific lessons at age three. He emphasises relaxation, proper breathing and visualisation exercises. The development of the ear is paramount. Thus the piece to be learned is always played before the lesson and memorised by the child. Older students study the music visually before they go to sleep. All students are taught "internal singing" - hearing the music in their mind's ear.

All the methods mentioned here rely on learning at two levels of consciousness - a wide awake (beta) level and a relaxed (alpha) level and learning both via active and passive phases.

Nonetheless, the Accelerated Learning method described later goes beyond the dual principles of previous researchers and extends into a series of very specific and practical *co-ordinated* techniques.

School can inhibit

Education **used** to be holistic

In the Middle Ages, Music was taught in Relation to Maths

GRAMMAR connected with LITERATURE

Information should be given in rich context of connections

Industrial revolution is partly to blame

le chat l'escalier
le chien bonjour L
la porte
l'hotel
arrives tomber

Dr Lozanov test – How many foreign words can be taught in one day?

FRENCH

92% correct at 100 words per day
96% correct at 200 words per day
96% correct at 1000 words per day
EXPECT MORE — GET MORE

Education for assembly line — like robots

skirt the barriers of the mind instead of frontal attack

Don't mention number of words —

1000 WORDS

until the goal has already been achieved

Instant Coffee

Lazy or a way of spending time with the family?

TOWN

Underlined towns remembered better

Double your reading speed in 20 minutes

The medium is the key. Emotion, body language, intonation communicate better than words

Accelerated Learning halves absenteeism and stress. School becomes enjoyable

147

THE STATE OF THE ART

When we set out to investigate Accelerated Learning some four years ago, many educators were trying to reproduce the methods and results of Dr. Lozanov. Yet his methods were already 15 years old. In the last four years the movement has progressed rapidly.

We found that while none of the recent discoveries about how the human brain and memory works, in any way contradicted Lozanov's principles, there were clear pointers to important areas of development and improvement.

In particular, we frequently heard the comment that Lozanov's methods, when applied to foreign language teaching, were unrivalled for the fast creation of large amounts of vocabulary - but they were less good at teaching grammar. Moreover, Lozanov had heavily emphasised the authority of the teacher as being an important element. This authority flowed from the fact that he or she *was* the teacher. Yet this made for passivity in the classroom. We, in contrast, had come to the conclusion that *active* involvement was perhaps the most important element in a class. The teacher's authority should flow from her manifest ability, not her titular role. Lozanov had also heavily emphasised the role of music (sound association) and it seemed reasonable to ask if there was enough imagery (visual association) in his original version of Accelerated Learning (The version described by Peter Kline in Chapter 7.)

In March, 1984, we had assembled enough information from our investigations to produce an inventory of the elements that would have to be built into an ideal Accelerated Learning Course. The inventory was compiled from our findings on how the brain and memory works, (the subject of Chapters 1-5), from our discussions with Accelerated Learning practitioners from Eastern Europe, Western Europe and the Americas and from our discussions with three consultants on the Accelerated Learning

Movement - Dr. Win Wenger, Paul Hollander and Charles Schmid. It is to the work of the first two that we now turn. We shall then be ready to draw all the threads together.

Articulate!

Win Wenger is an independent lecturer who specialises in certain key aspects of Accelerated Learning. He acknowledges the success of the Lozanov method but points out that it is comparatively weak on the use of visuals and visualisation. Whereas Lozanov's emphasis has been on creating memory, Win Wenger's emphasis is on drawing out that memory and on ways to facilitate subsequent and spontaneous recall. After all, he says the word "Education" is derived from the Latin "educare", which literally means "drawing out". And you can only draw out what is already in there!

I found the time I spent in Win Wenger's company exciting and I acknowledge that it stimulated us to think about some key improvements that have now been built into the new version of Accelerated Learning.

Win Wenger comes back time and again to the thought that we already know much more than we think we do. He starts with a philosophical point. The human body is almost entirely replaced every seven years, so the essence of you is not physical, it is your personality. Your personality is effectively a pattern, a behaviour style combined with your unique knowledge and experiences.

Socrates was the first teacher to confirm that the task of an educator was to draw out information already within the student and thereby to let people teach themselves. Consequently Socrates believed that the main function of a teacher was to teach people to *articulate*. Articulation not only draws forth existing information, but if you articulate information that is new to you (i.e. describe it in detail out loud) that very act of description sharpens your perception of the subject. It also facilitates and deepens your memory of it.

You can readily prove the point. Take a moment now and stare at some quiet common object in the room. Start describing it out loud and you will discover all sorts of features in it you never consciously noticed before. We know that the richer the detail you construct and, therefore the more associations you form, the easier it is to remember.

Why should the act of articulation have such a very positive effect on memory? *'That's easy'* answered Dr. Wenger, *'I believe that as much as 80% of the brains function is visual. Visualisation involves the subconscious. If you read something new and then close your eyes and describe it out loud, you by definition are synchronising the activity of your left and right brain - because visualisation is a right brain function and speech is a left brain function. Articulation, therefore, which involves whole brain activity, is a vital element in fast learning.*

'I would go further. Articulation is essential to understanding. Let me give an example. Bernstein at Harvard University believes there may be as many as 4 million colours. However, there are fewer than 200 words for colours so there are for all practical purposes, fewer than 200 colours. If you can't articulate something it effectively doesn't exist!'

Bernstein conducted another series of tests with wide implications. He took two groups of young children. One group was educationally severely disadvantaged, with a poor vocabulary. The other group was normally educated. He showed pictures of butterflies to both groups. The butterflies included several different species; some were patterned, some were striped, some had dots of colour on their wings. The children who lacked the words for "stripe" or "dot", literally could not draw these particular butterflies. Without the words their ability to see and understand the relevant concept was strictly limited. Yet when they were subsequently taught the words, they could then draw the correct shapes.

From these thoughts, Win Wenger has produced some impressive ways to improve your ability to visualise, to form images and to develop your power of observation. Nevertheless his simplest concept is perhaps the strongest. Whenever you close your eyes, visualise the subject and articulate that image out loud, you have achieved a left/right brain symbiosis and a fast route into memorisation.

Different Strokes for Different Folks

Paul Hollander, an educational specialist and a consultant to IBM on the advantages and principles of Accelerated Learning, has also been influential on the format in which we have finally produced Accelerated Learning for home use.

Paul Hollander insisted that we needed to recognise the fact that everyone has a preferred learning style and that each Accelerated Learning course should allow for this.

Sensory Systems

Within the last 5-6 years a number of researchers have established the importance of three principle forms of communication between human beings, and demonstrated that these communication styles are mirrored by learning styles.

The principle researchers have been Richard Bandler and John Grinder whose book "Frogs into Princes" has become a classic in the field; Dilts "Neuro-Linguistic Programming" (NLP); and Zaner-Bloser who published a major report entitled "Teaching through Modality Strength". These books were published in 1979 and the techniques are now generally known as NLP.

The main conclusion was that each person has a dominant sensory system. Thus you may prefer to communicate or learn in either:-

A Visual Way - (you are orientated to visualise)

An Auditory Way - (you normally like to hear presentations or talk out problems)

A Kinaesthetic Way - (kinaesthetic means "to do with movement, active, action orientated").

The initials V.A.K. will be used as a shorthand, (Visual, Auditory, Kinaesthetic).

At first sight the analysis may seem obvious - but the implications are significant. If you want to communicate with someone who is highly visual, she will find a lesson that consists only of an audio tape tedious and unsatisfying. Conversely, an auditory learner will benefit less from a presentation that relies purely on slides. Note we are **NOT** saying that you communicate or learn only with your preferred sense. Clearly we all process information by visual, auditory *and* kinaesthetic means.

We are saying, however, that learning will be easier and more effective if the elements are expressed in the way you prefer to learn, whether that is V. A. or K.

How you present something is often as important as what you say - and indeed may determine whether it is understood at all.

Psychologist Robert Mehrabian has conducted studies to determine which of 3 elements are the most important in communication during conversation. He asked respondents to predict the relative importance of each and then gave them the *actual* measured importance. Here are the results:-

	Predicted Influence	Actual Influence
Verbal Content i.e. words alone	50%	7%
Vocal Influence i.e. tone, stress, accent pitch, pauses, silences.	20% } 50%	38% } 93%
Non Verbal Influence Expression, touching gestures, posture, distance.	30%	55%

The medium really is the message!

How to Find your own Preferred Learning Style

There are two main ways. The first is simplistic, but surprisingly accurate. It has to do with the way you habitually express yourself.

The chart below will help you relate your normal expressions to your preferred sensory style.

VISUAL LEARNERS - will typically say:-
"I *see* now"
"That *looks* right to me"
"I need to get it into *perspective*"
"I'm in the dark about..."
"I get the *picture*"
"That's an *enlightening* answer"
"I can *picture* that"

AUDITORY LEANERS - will typically say:-
"That *sounds* right"
"That *rings* a bell"
"Suddenly it *clicked*"
"Just *listen* to me"
"I get *tuned* into it"
"I *hear* what you say"
"Something *tells* me that's the answer"
"That's *music* to my ears"
"I can *hear* you're unhappy"

KINAESTHETIC LEARNERS - will typically say:-

"That *feels* right"

"It's an *intense* problem"

"It's a *smooth* answer to a *tough* problem!"

"Give me a *concrete* example"

"I'm *groping* for an answer"

"I have a *firm grip* on the subject"

"I find it difficult to *handle*"

By matching the teaching approach with the preferred learning approach, we are able to establish a more direct, sympathetic and clear communication. In a real sense, the teacher and pupil are "speaking the same language".

You can establish your dominant sensory system somewhat more specifically by considering the following list and asking which characteristic most represents your personal preferences.

PREFERRED SENSORY STYLE

WHEN YOU		VISUAL	AUDITORY	KINAESTHETIC
SPELL	do you	try to see the word	use the phonetic approach	write the word down to find if it "feels" right.
VISUALISE	do you	see vivid detailed pictures	think in sounds	have few images. those that you do have, involve movement.
ARE CONCENTRATING	do you	get distracted by untidiness or movement	get distracted by sounds/ noises	get distracted by movement.
ARE ANGRY	do you	become silent and seethe	express it in an outburst	storm off, grit your teeth, clench your fists.
FORGET SOMETHING	do you	forget names but remember faces	forget faces but remember names	remember best what you did.
CONTACT PEOPLE ON BUSINESS	do you	prefer a direct, personal meeting face to face	prefer the telephone	talk it out whilst walking or during another activity.
ARE RELAXING	do you	prefer to watch T.V., read, see a play.	prefer to listen to the radio/play records.	prefer to play sports/games.

	do you		
ENJOY THE ARTS	do you	like paintings	like music	like dancing
REWARD SOMEONE	do you	write remarks of praise on their work or in a note.	given them oral praise	give them a pat on the back
TRY TO INTERPRET SOMEONE'S MOOD	do you	primarily look at their facial expression	listen to their tone of voice	watch their body movements
ARE READING	do you	like descriptive scenes/stop to imagine the scene/Take little notice of pictures.	enjoy dialogue and conversation 'Hear' the characters talk	prefer action stories or are not a keen reader
LEARN	do you	like to see demonstrations, diagrams, slides, posters.	like verbal instructions, talks and lectures.	prefer direct involvement - learning through activities/role playing, etc.
ARE INACTIVE	do you	look around, doodle, watch something	talk to yourself or other people	fidget
ARE TALKING	do you	talk sparingly, but dislike listening for too long	enjoy listening but are impatient to talk	gesture a lot and use expressive movements

It would be very unusual if your answers fell only in one column, because we are discussing, not exclusive communication and learning styles, but preferred learning styles.

The practical purpose of being able to identify learning styles and preferred sensory systems is to ensure that the ideal learning programme communicates to the learner in all three "modes'.

In this way the learning process will involve the maximum sensory input, and we know that this makes for rich, detailed associations and hence fast memory creation. Moreover, each student will feel comfortable, because one or more of the learning activities is in the style with which he feels most in sympathy.

The extremes of preference, of course, are the artist, the

musician and the dancer, and it is clear how you would present information to each one, i.e.

> I *see* your point
>> or
> I *tune* into your argument
>> or
> I *feel* at home with your presentation.

Eye movement clues

It is a curious, and rather charming fact, that we all give off involuntary clues as to the sort of sensory system we prefer to employ or are employing at the moment.

Most attention has been placed on eye movement, because it is the easiest to detect. In fact breathing patterns, muscle tone, vocal tone and, of course, gestures all signal our individual style of communication.

Given a normal right handed person, you will find that their eyes move in a set manner, in response to the six main types of questions. Let's look at these six questions and the reaction they elicit.

TYPICAL QUESTION	RESPONSE	CODE
1. When did you last see the Queen on T.V.?	Subject recalls an actual image i.e. remembers a specific scene (visual recall)	Vr
2. Can you picture an elephant riding a bicycle?	Subject constructs an image he has never seen before (visual construct)	Vc
3. What is your favourite song - how does it start?	Subject recalls an actual sound(s) (auditory recall)	Ar
4. Can you imagine the sound of a bath running while your telephone is ringing?	Subject constructs a sound he has probably not heard before (auditory construct)	Ac

156

5. Think out the two main principles of Accelerated Learning you've learned so far and how you would present the argument to some friends at a dinner party.

Subject is holding an internal conversation or dialogue with himself (auditory dialogue) — Ad

6. How does it feel when you stroke a cat?

Subject recalls an actual sensation - a Kinaesthetic experience. It can be feel, taste, smell. (Kinaesthetic) — K

If you ask people the above six types of question, their eyes will normally move in the following way. (It is the last shift before they look back at you again that is significant). The movements are depicted as you face the subject.

Visual recall - eyes move up and to your right

Visual Construct - eyes move up and to your left

Auditory recall - eyes move sideways to your right

Auditory Construct - eyes move sideways to your left

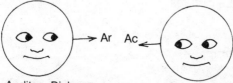

Auditory Dialogue - eyes move down and to the right

Kinaesthetic - eyes move down and left.

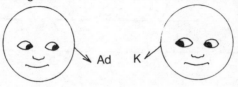

We can superimpose the six positions for the eye clues on one face to summarise the indicators of the mode in which your partner, or pupil is thinking.

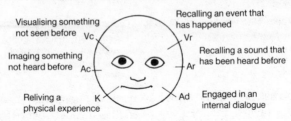

Visualising something not seen before Vc

Recalling an event that has happened Vr

Imaging something not heard before Ac

Recalling a sound that has been heard before Ar

Reliving a physical experience K

Engaged in an internal dialogue Ad

Psychologists have found that these eye movement clues hold good in almost every culture in Europe, Africa and America. (Although for some extraordinary reason the Basque people in North East Spain do not respond typically!)

In addition a dilation of the pupils and a defocussing of the eyes is normally a sign that the person is processing thoughts internally and may well be visualising.

Generally, these eye movement patterns will be reversed for left handed people. Although the patterns are not necessarily true for all right handed persons, nevertheless people who do not follow the above pattern will have a consistent pattern of their own.

Why not practice the set of eye clues below. Match up the statements with the eye clues and put the correct code underneath the pictures.

Eye Clues

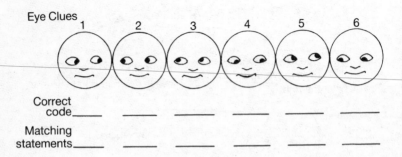

1   2   3   4   5   6

Correct
code____ ____ ____ ____ ____ ____

Matching
statements____ ____ ____ ____ ____ ____

Statements:

A. Let me consider how this affects me
B. I remember he used those exact words
C. I feel really happy
D. She really looked good in that dress
E. I'm trying to imagine how it might work
F. Let me tell you how a politician might express it.

Answers:

Picture	1	2	3	4	5	6
Correct code	Ar	Ac	Vc	Ad	Vr	K
Matching statement	B	F	E	A	D	C

The Significance of other Body Language

Psychologists have observed other characteristics that also indicate the individuals dominant sensory system. Breathing is especially indicative.

Thus it is common to observe:-

	Visual	Auditory	Kinaesthetic
Breathing	Tends to be shallow in upper chest	Tends to be even in mid chest	Tends to be very full using lower stomach
Posture	Tends to tense shoulders, neck to hunch.	Tension is evenly distributed over shoulders and back. Head is often to one side.	Generally relaxed posture
Voice	Characteristically, rapid speech	Even pace, good clear enuciation	Slower spoken, longer pauses, deeper pitch

How do Sensory Preferences Affect Learning?

The above analysis has already begun to influence teaching styles to a significant extent.

For example, it has been discovered that good spellers

invariably bring to mind an image of the word (V), and can 'feel' (K) if it is right. Bad spellers don't use this sequence. They try to check the word phonetically and with English that is a poor predictor of correct spelling!

Consequently it is much more productive to teach a bad speller the sequence of V + K, than it is to ask him or her laboriously to memorise the specific spelling of thousands of words. In other words you have taught the correct principle and that principle holds good in thousands of different situations.

It is important to repeat that no-one is a pure visual or pure auditory or pure kinaesthetic learner. However, we react *best* to our dominant system. So it pays to train yourself to develop your other senses, in order to maximise the beneficial effect of all the signals reaching you.

It should also be noted that each sensory channel (V.A.K.) has sub-divisions. For instance, the visual 'mode' can have colour, or black and white, can be two or three dimensional, and can involve movement. The Auditory mode has loudness, tone and pitch. Once you recognise your strengths and weaknesses you can practice for improvement - any improvement in imagining will improve your ability to learn.

Professional teachers, or people who regularly present to meetings, should take special note of the fact that, when you have presented a significant amount of new information, it is natural for the recipients to start to process that information internally - by looking up in a "visual construct" mode or down in an "auditory dialogue" mode.

To the presenter, this can look like inattention. Many lecturers will instinctively react by increasing the pace and volume of their talk in an attempt to force attention and 'hammer the point home'. The result is irritation and a lowering of understanding in the audience.

A better strategy would be to reduce pace. This allows the internal processing to take place and time for a recap.

A teacher who comes to recognise that she or he is a primarily visual communicator, will find a much better rapport if she deliberately introduces Auditory and Kinaesthetic elements into her teaching. Clashes in learning styles versus teaching styles often explain why a child can do poorly one year and then bloom the following year with a new teacher in the same subject.

There is a parallel in respect of left brain/right brain learning. Educational Researcher Bernice McCarthy in her book "The 4-Mat System" has identified four different types of learner.

The "Innovative" learner who is imaginative and relates new information to her or his own experiences.

The "Common Sense" learner who wants realistic examples relevant to real life.

The "Dynamic" learner who wants to learn by actual involvement and specific experiences.

The "Analytical" learner who wants to see the principles and concepts behind the subject.

Only the last type of learner is a natural left brain learner, who finds it comfortable to be verbal and logical and have an auditory presentation of information. The other three types are right brain individuals who will prefer a visual and kinesthetic approach.

Bernice McCarthy is of the opinion that the majority of students start off as right brain dominant - yet the majority of teachers instruct for left brain assimilation. No wonder conventional learning has been a strain!

The conclusion must be clear. The ideal learning method will orchestrate left and right brain activity and employ a full range of visual, auditory and kinesthetic activities to make learning comfortable and to invoke the maximum response.

It is now clear that someone whom we describe as naturally "sensitive", or with whom we have a natural "rapport", is probably only unconsciously communicating to us in the style we like best.

A group of psychotherapists have extended the principle of "rapport" into what is termed "matching" and "leading". When in the company of someone you like, talking at the same pace and tone and moving at the same tempo.

This is often done quite deliberately by a psychiatrist, who will first "match" his clients action, and then gradually "lead" them to a calmer tempo.

The use of Baroque music has a similar function - the relaxing tempo of the music produces a matching physical and mental response in the listener and leads them into a state of relaxed receptivity. Bandler and Grinder - following the work of the brilliant psychotherapists Milton Erickson and Virginia Satir - have evolved a useful technique you can easily use yourself.

It is deceptively simple, and indeed most people's initial reaction is that it is too simplistic to work - but it does.

They asked each member of their class to remember and describe a time when they experienced real pleasure and delight in learning something. It may have been riding a bicycle, suddenly understanding the solution to a problem, or having something explained that was new and really interesting - something they personally felt was fascinating. As the subject recounts this pleasurable experience, a clear change comes over them. Their breathing rate, heart rate, voice tone and often skin colour and posture changes. They have recaptured their original enthusiasm. If the psychotherapist, for example, now touches the individual's wrist or shoulder, their state of mind becomes associated with that signal or as it is termed "anchored". Later that same state of mind can be recaptured by simply triggering the "anchor" - i.e. touching the wrist or shoulder.

It does sound difficult to accept initially but our sub-conscious is simplistic. We find the technique worth repeating for two reasons.

First you can do it for yourself and thereby bring back in an enthusiasm and feeling of pleasurable anticipation for a learning session.

Secondly it is yet further proof that even our deepest and apparently sub-conscious beliefs were once learned and if we choose, can be brought to the surface and changed.

A Specific Learning Pattern

An excellent book on the latest psychology of teaching is "Master Teaching" written by Bernard F. Cleveland.

He has shown that we can each develop a learning sequence that is ideal for us personally. The following sequence incorporates what we have discovered to date and formalises it into a learning sequence. For each new subject you would -

Read the text and *visualise* the contents

Hear the words internally in your 'mind's ear'.

Feel the text, or act out the key elements or in some way physically involve yourself.

Using the new expressions we have learned, the sequences might be:

V   - read material
Vr - recall it visually - image it
A   - hear a verbal presentation
Ar - hear the material in your head, rehearse it
Vc - construct a *new* image of the subject in your head, visualise it vividly.
K   - Act out the subject or underline key words
V+K Write out key words in your favourite colour. Draw a picture or map. Write some of the words backwards. Walk around while you read or listen.
Ad- Present the argument to an imaginary audience.

Involve your senses and you will involve your subconscious. Involve your subconscious, and you have the most powerful part of your brain helping in the learning process.

NOTE Workshops and tuition in the subjects covered in this chapter are available from F. G. Gatti-Doyle (co-author of *Accelerated Learning Italian Language Course*), Valerie Beeby and Peter Gardiner. For further information please send stamped addressed envelope to *Mens Sana*, 26 Belvedere Square, London SW19 5DJ. Telephone or Fax: 081 947 0844.

PUTTING IT ALL TOGETHER

In the four years it took to research this book we learnt a great deal about the mind, memory and learning. Quite deliberately we approached it from the psychologist's standpoint rather than the existing educator, because this was more likely to produce the fresh thinking that every genuine breakthrough must have.

The time has come to recap on what we have learnt. In doing so, some important principles will emerge. These principles direct us towards an ideal learning programme. They also pinpoint how it is possible to improve upon the proven success and strength of the Lozanov method.

For reasons that are given later, we have made some of our conclusions relevant to the teaching of languages - since this is the least easy learning situation of all.

What we learned
1. Your brain has enormous potential. It is capable of much more than you have imagined. In fact the more you use it the more associations and connections you make and the easier it is to remember and learn yet more new material. A rich, stimulating environment is the main factor in achieving full potential in youngsters and preventing deterioration in old age.

2. The left and right halves of the brain process information in somewhat different ways. The right brain responds to art, music and patterns - it processes information holistically, grasps the whole picture quickly and is more sensitive to subconscious influences. The left brain tends to work on a step by step basis. Yet most existing teaching is directed to the left brain.

    Fully involve the right brain and you don't just double your brain power, you increase it many times over.

3. Relaxation is important to create a stress free learning environment and conditions of ideal receptivity. Relaxation is associated with a predominantly Alpha brain wave pattern. Relaxation releases energy for learning.

4. All new information enters the short term memory store, but only gets transferred to the long term memory store if it is rehearsed immediately.

5. Registering new facts depends on strong encoding, strong encoding depends to a large extent on creating strong associations.

   Strong encoding is achieved by creating concrete images of sights, feelings, sounds, taste and smell. The stronger the original encoding the better the ultimate recall - just as the better the index, the more usable is the library.

   Recall is essential to learning and recall is different to, and less easy to achieve than, recognition.

6. Words linked to pictures are easier to learn/remember because you have achieved dual encoding. Recall depends on association, linking ideas together in a pattern.

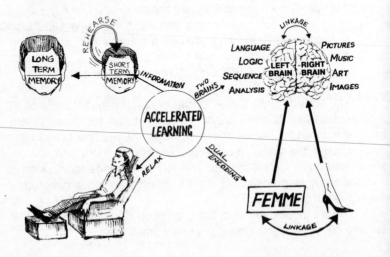

7. Visual memory is essentially perfect. The key to memory (and learning) is, therefore, to improve your visualisation and to form strong *visual* associations for new material. Interactive visual images are the most powerful. That's the lesson from mnemonics.

8. Basically the more time you spend learning the better the learning. However, the way the time is deployed is highly influential. 'Distributed practice' is the optimum strategy. An ideal learning pattern would involve:

(a) Immediate rehearsal within the short term memory span.

(b) A test after a few minutes.

(c) A review after the first hour.

(d) A short review after an overnight rest, because sleep appears to reinforce memory.

(e) A short review after a week.

(f) A short review after a month.

Such a schedule can maintain recall at up to 88% - four times better than the expected curve of forgetting.

9. Individual lessons should have breaks. It utilises the Primary, Recency and Zeigarnik effects.

10. Lessons should ideally incorporate something outstanding in the middle to raise arousal - the "Von Restorf" effect.

11. Teach the specifics first - in languages the descriptive nouns and verbs are easiest to learn.

12. The mind naturally imposes organisation on new material and groups ideas or words together. This process helps memory. Even sorting words out into categories is a significant memory aid. (Tulving)

13. Learning the principle is easier than learning each individual example. (Teach bad speller to visualise).

14. Meaning is vital to memory - which is why nonsense phrases are so difficult to learn. There is no relationship available.

15. Context is important. It provides an overview a 'map' of what you will learn and facilitates meaning. A jigsaw is easier to do if you can see the whole picture.

16. Learning by example is better than learning by rote - but the more general the examples the easier it is to apply the knowledge later in a broad set of circumstances.

17. Chunking is an important aid to memory.
18. Rhythm and Rhyme are important aids to memory. They stir body reaction and they are a form of organised pattern which makes it easier to remember.
19. Music, especially Baroque Music, is an ideal accompaniment to new material. It ensures left/right brain linkage, creates an auditory and rhythmic association with the material, creates an emotive link with the material and simultaneously promotes a state of relaxed awareness, by "leading".
20. Memory works by creating a network of associated ideas. A Memory Map reproduces very closely the way in which the brain works - so it facilitates learning.
21. Individual words are less easy to remember than ideas or sentences, which are again forms of organisation, so linking words together helps. Hence it is easier to learn a language via stories - each new word building on, and linking to, the vocabulary already learned.
22. We probably all have the potential for photographic memory. The key to it is imagination.
23 Suggestion can improve acutal performance greatly - not by creating new abilities but by unblocking the negative suggestion that something cannot be done.
   These negative suggestions are often formed in childhood. When a suggestion is implanted in the subconscious mind, the subconscious mind will find a way of bringing it about. Suggestion is a powerful tool for learning. Creating a belief in success and a positive self-image, will, when allied to a sound and realistic learning programme, create great success. The subconscious mind appears to be controlled by the limbic system and is best accessed and influenced, not by left brain logic, but by an approach that incorporates an emotive appeal.
24. Learning is maximised when all the elements are focussed on the learning process. Since possibly up to 90% of communication is at the subconscious level, the greater the number of subconscious stimuli that are orchestrated to aid learning, the faster and more effective is that learning. Such learning has been characterised as intuitive learning. Some

ways this can be achieved (in a language course for example) are:-

(a) By using a side by side presentation of the text which takes advantage of peripheral vision.

(b) By using a soft female voice which reproduces a secure learning environment.

(c) By incorporating background music with which the voice of the teacher can harmonise. This appeals to the subconscious through rhythm and through emotive associations.

(d) By playing games, and acting out roles, which distract your attention and allows information to be indirectly and subconsciously assimilated.

(e) By providing information on cards and posters around the room which is subconsciously noted and stored.

(f) By teaching in stories the grammar can be indirectly absorbed.

25. Imaging and articulation of new material is a powerful memory creating device.

26. Presenting each lesson to the student in the three sensory channels - Visual, Auditory and Kinaesthetic - ensures that the presentation is in a style in which the student learns best, and that all three senses are co-ordinated to make learning highly effective. It also enables the student to deliberately extend the use of his senses.

27. The above programme ensures early success and thus provides the motivation for extra attention and *involvement*. This fuels a virtuous circle.

We are almost ready to draw our conclusions together and to describe an Accelerated Learning procedure that will work for you at home, in your business life, and to help your child progress at school.

The method will work for any subject - maths, English literature, geography, history, physics. We have chosen, however, to describe the techniques as it applies to languages, since learning a language is the most demanding of all learning situations.

We have seen that no learning can take place without memory and memory depends to a great extent on creating strong associations. A memorable event in your life is invariably linked or associated with a physical feeling and/or with a strong visual image, and/or with your surroundings at the time. The reason why scientists who research memory, routinely use nonsense phrases in their experimental work, is that such phrases, by definition, do not mean anything. They, therefore, trigger no associations in the mind. Consequently nonsense phrases are the least easy things to memorise.

At the beginning a foreign language is rather like a list of nonsense phrases. There are no associations to 'hook' on to.

The importance of association in language is easy to demonstrate. For example, the German for dog is HUND. that is an easy word to learn because you have a simple association to the familiar English word HOUND. But you would take longer to learn the German for SUCCESS which is ERFOLG - because it has no linguistic association for you. It triggers no connection.

If Accelerated Learning can boost the speed and effectiveness of learning a language by three or more times, then it will obviously work proportionally even better for other subjects.

Before we finally look at the construction of an actual Accelerated Learning Language Course, it will be helpful to briefly review the works of two people acknowledged as among the world's leading authorities on the teaching of languages. Earl Stevick and Stephen Krashen.

Earl W. Stevick has recently retired as Professor at the School of Language Studies Foreign Service Institute, Arlington, Virginia. His book "Memory, Meaning and Method" which drew together a life time's experience in surveying teaching methods and in practical teaching, has become a classic.

Some of his conclusions are already echoed in this book, but one in particular is worth highlighting.

"Involvement"

Time after time in Stevick's work you came across the overriding importance of involvement. Sometimes he refers to it as 'personal investment', sometimes as 'depth of processing', but it comes to the same thing - you remember and learn what you became involved in.

There is a Chinese proverb that aptly sums up Stevick's philosophy:

"I forget what I hear
I remember what I see
I learn what I do".

We have already referred to the work of Kintsch and Bowen, but Stevick quotes a further study by leading memory researcher J. Craik. Craik gave his subjects a list of words to be learned. He then asked four types of questions.

1. Is it printed in capital letters or lower case type?
2. What does it rhyme with?
3. What category of word does it belong to - is it a colour, or an animal, or a household object?
4. Could it fit into the following sentence?

Each question required the subject to think about the word but at increasing levels of depth. The deeper processing took some little extra time, but the results "were dramatically better" in terms of recall.

Craik ascribes the results to the fact that the extra involvement ensured that the words were indeed passed from the primary or short term memory store into the long term memory.

The message from Craik's work and from this book in general is loud, and it is clear, and it is also good news.

Parrot fashion repetition does not work. It is a superficial use of words. A relaxed involvement in your subject via interesting activities and games that require *COMMUNICATION* does work. That is the route to Accelerated Learning and it is why, when we devised our Language Programmes, we chose to teach via stories, and by real life dialogues, in which the learner literally acts out the roles.

In a review of learning methods that have incorporated the principle of involvement, Stevick picks out four in particular:-

1. **Total Physical Response,** developed by V. N. Asher, concentrated especially on teaching pupils by commands from the earliest stage. Commands demanded a response and thus involvement. Passivity does not create the best environment for learning - but committed activity does. The more arousal you create in the learner the better. As

researcher J. B. Brierly noted *'What is important and emotionally charged, is more rapidly embedded than that which is neutral.'*

Tests by Kleinsmith and Kaplan as early as 1963, showed that high arousal words were three times better remembered than neutral words - so pairing high arousal words with more neutral words becomes a good strategy in teaching a language. In psychological terms the strategy ensures that the limbic system and the new brain are interacting and that turns on the full power of the brain.

2. **"Liberated Spanish"** developed by Keith Saucer of Fresno USA. His first step is to teach the vocabulary of disagreement. In this way he automatically engages the involvement of his students, because an argument produces arousal.

3. **"Community Language Learning"** or C.L.L. developed by leading language researcher C. A. Curran. One of Currans's primary techniques is to create a circle of pupils and a warm friendly atmosphere. He then tape records statements made by the students in the new language. This tape is played back and analysed. The process again automatically involves the participants since they are listening to their own voices.

Curran is particularly adept at phrasing questions in a way that provokes involvement. Thus "describe Mary" (a character in a story) is not nearly as involving as "say what you like, or what you dislike, about Mary."

4. **The Silent Way** by Caleb Gattegno, which greatly emphasises the learner and subordinates the role of the teacher. We cannot do justice to the technique here, but in essence, the class is given a very limited initial vocabulary. They would typically be taught the word for a rod (a round coloured piece of wood). Then the teacher acts out all the words while he says the sentence 'take the rod' or 'give the rod to me' in the target language.

The pupils' task is to figure out what the words must mean. The act of figuring it out is involvement.

Subsequently vocabulary is built up by linking new words and ideas on the previously learned vocabulary.

All of the above four teaching approaches, (each one of which is much more sophisticated than the short extract given here may imply), have a common and vital thread. They demand involvement. If you want to learn fast and learn well, you must achieve the same.

There is, finally, one other specialist sense in which you need to involve yourself in learning a language - one to which Peter O'Connell had already referred. Your own language and nationality is very much bound up with your sense of identity, your ego. Unfortunately to integrate too completely with a new culture can be threatening.

H. W. Seligen writing in "Language Sciences" in 1975 noted that people who learned to pronounce a new language with the least accent tended to have had few friends in their immediate peer group as children. They were, therefore, quite happy to take on a new identity. Revealingly actor Peter Sellers alluded to the same factor when he was asked to comment on his outstanding ability for mimicry.

If you are generally sensitive to the feelings of others you will find the acquisition of a good foreign accent comparatively easy. *'Empathy'* notes Psychologist A. Z. Guiora *'predicts pronunciation ability.'* The more rigid the personality, the less easy it is to acquire an authentic accent.

The way to achieve a good accent is to involve yourself (that word again!) in the role of a character in your new language, imagining how he or she would feel and talk, using appropriate gestures and facial expressions. Return to a childlike readiness to be receptive, adaptive and spontaneous, and you'll succeed, not just in learning the vocabulary, but in learning the accent too.

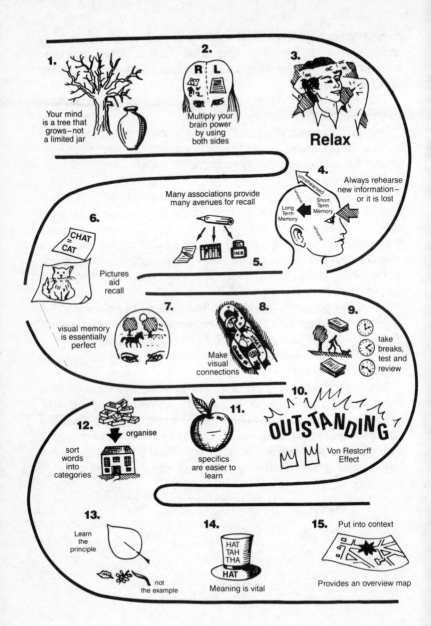

174

16.

✓
1 x 2 = 2
2 x 2 = 4
3 x 2 = 6
4 x 2 = 8
5 x 2 = 10

Learning by example better than by note

17.

CHUNK

chunking is an important aid

18.

Rhythm & Rhyme

Words that chime & beat in time

19.

Baroque Music creates auditory and rhythmic association

20.

MEMORY MAP

Memory maps mimic the mind & facilitate learning

21.

Language easier to learn via story

STORIES IN ANOTHER LANGUAGE

ONCE UPON A TIME

22.

Use your photographic memory

23.

Use suggestion

24.

90% of communication is at sub-conscious level. Peripheral

conscious vision

music games

stories posters

Peripheral

vision

25.

CHAPEAU

Image & Articulate

26.

VAK

V
A
K

Use all the senses

27.

Accelerated Learning

VIRTUOUS CIRCLE

Early success

175

FIRST RELAX!

We live at an exciting point in history. There is an exponential growth in new ideas, new products, new discoveries. Never before have we been called upon to change so many of our habits, beliefs, opinions and so much of our life style.

To some people it represents a welcome and exhilarating challenge. To others it brings a high level of stress and anxiety.

The toll of this anxiety and stress is rising hypertension, heart attacks, strokes, insomnia. Stress related disease is the fastest rising category of illness in the Western World.

We have always lived with stress, but modern humanity has no easy physical escape. Unlike our primitive ancestors, who might be forced to fight, but who could then run away to relax and recover, we often remain in a state of anxiety and tension. Our nervous system is constantly aroused, but we are unable to resolve the tension by either "fight or flight".

Dr. Hans Seyle, who is a director of the Institute of Experimental Surgery at the University of Montreal has shown that unrelieved stress produces hormonal imbalances.

These can lead to high blood pressure. Additionally the hormonal changes can produce lesions in the walls of the arteries. The body tries to repair these by building up cholesterol plaque, but this can in turn produce a hardening of the arteries and a further increase in blood pressure.

Dr. Seyle's real discovery, however, is that unrelieved stress supresses the immune system, which is responsible for fighting and destroying viruses and cancer.

These important findings have been supported by a study at the University of New South Wales, which showed that bereavement lowered the body's immune response. Dr. Humphrey at the British Medical Council was also able to demonstrate that the body's immunity to tuberculosis was significantly affected by hypnotic suggestion.

The physiology of the process may have been explained by Dr. George Solomon of California State University. He showed that incisions in the hypothalamus lead to a suppression of the immune system. The hypothalamus affects the endocrine production in the body, and the hypothalamus is part of the limbic system, identified as being largely the seat of our emotions and subconscious reactions.

For the first time then, we have a well supported theory that shows how the mind and the emotions, can directly affect our health for good and for ill. The reduction of stress is not only conducive for better learning, it is literally vital for well-being.

So how can we overcome state of unresolved arousal? One of the most efficient ways is to learn the simple technique of deep breathing and relaxation. When our muscles are relaxed, the brain receives a signal that all is well, and arousal is lowered.

Strenuous exercise and sport also releases excess muscle tension - but pure physical activity is rarely enough for full relaxation. We do, however, recommend that you do a few minutes gentle exercise and breathing at any time of the day in the kitchen, office or work place - because it undoubtedly does help to prevent tension, headaches and neckaches.

Young children learn easily and without effort or strain because it is spontaneous. Later, as we have seen, we grow to expect learning to be more of a problem, to require effort. The result is an instinctive tensing of the body, a tightening of the jaw, a change in the chemistry of the nervous system - in other words tension.

The ideal way to approach learning is the way you'd approach a music concert. You would be calm, with a pleasurable anticipation, ready to let it happen. This approach is not passive because, although you are not yourself making the music, the music is working on your mind, creating moods, ideas, and associations. One form of creativity producing another.

The following relaxation technique has the specific objective of creating pleasurable anticipation and a calm receptivity. It has been refined over several years to be easy to learn and fast to take effect.

The technique is called Awareness Relaxation. It enables you to focus your awareness on your body and breathing, becoming aware alternately of tension and release.

As a simple example, make a fist with your hand. Tighten your fist and lower arm. Hold that tension and be aware of the feeling. Make it tighter. Then release your fist, relax your hand and take a full deep breath. Feel the tension flow from the hand as you breathe out. Be aware of all the sensations in your hand and lower arm. This is the physical awareness of your body's tension that you will learn.

Breathing

Correct breathing is the first step in Awareness Relaxation. Deep breathing from the diaphragm is the key to relaxation. It is the breathing used in the practice of meditation, in Yoga, and in relaxation during childbirth. A full deep breath increases the amount of oxygen as the body begins to function efficiently, especially during mental activity.

When a full, deep, intake of breath is taken, the diaphragm moves down to create a vacuum in the lung cavity and pushes out the abdomen. To feel the effect place your hand over your navel and imagine you have a balloon in your stomach. Breathe deeply through the nose, filling the balloon. Feel the balloon inflate and your hand move outwards. The further your hand moves, the deeper you have drawn air into the bottom of your lungs. Breathe as deeply as possible but without overbreathing. If you find breathing difficult through the nose, breathe through your mouth, but always draw the air into the bottom of the lungs.

As you breathe out, imagine the balloon deflating and feel the abdomen falling. Your out-breath should take longer than inhaling, and be accompanied by a slight sigh, because this sigh also helps to release tension.

After breathing in, hold the breath for 2 to 4 seconds, then exhale and again hold the breath for 2 to 4 seconds. Become aware of this precise moment of stillness and how easily the mind can focus on a single idea. Also remember this quiet relaxed moment when you are next in a stressful situation.

If you practice slow deep breathing, you will also find that your ability to relax increases and your heart rate will decrease. It will no longer be necessary to follow a conscious breathing pattern.

Instead just allow your body to become automatically and naturally relaxed during the concert sessions. The music will automatically create the right frame of mind for easy absorbtion of material. You will find that your breathing will follow the rhythm of the music.

You can reach a wonderful relaxed state with the following simple procedure.

1. Imagine the balloon in your abdomen. Feel it inflate when breathing in, feel it deflate when breathing out.
2. Breathe in. Be aware of the air flowing in as the balloon is filling.
3. Breathe out gently, with a long sigh as the balloon deflates.
4. Pause.
5. Breathe in. Be aware of the air filling your lungs.
6. Hold it.
7. Breathe out with a sigh. Feel the warm air leave your body.
8. Pause.
9. Breathe in. Be aware of the air flowing in.
10. Hold it.
11. Breathe out with a sigh and feel the tension draining away.
12. Pause.

Before starting any exercise on relaxation always take three full deep breaths and feel the tension drain away on the outbreath.

Try it now and prove it for yourself.

Body exercises

A few extra, simple exercises involving gentle movement and stretching, will help the muscles relax and will also help to relieve a great deal of tension.

Begin the exercises in a standing position and take three deep slow breaths, exhaling with a long sigh and allowing yourself to relax on the outbreath.

(1) **Shoulder and neck exercise**

Your shoulders and neck carry a lot of tension, particularly if you drive long distances, or work at a desk all day.

Let your arms hang loose. Pull down your shoulders, feel them drop. Then pull them down even further.

Rotate your shoulders.

Let your arms hang loose, rotate the shoulders forward. Roll them up and down in large circles. Hunch them up towards your neck. Now reverse the rotation, rolling them up and backwards in a circle. Do as many rotations as is comfortable. Try and rotate just the shoulders - not the arms.

Take a deep breath and exhale with a sigh.

Bend your shoulders.

1. Put your hands on your thighs and push your shoulders forward. Cave in your chest. Feel the movement around the neck and shoulders. Pull back the shoulders. Repeat as many times as is comfortable.

2. Bend your shoulders back. Try to bring the shoulder blades together. Do this as many times as is comfortable. Take three deep breaths.

Neck rotation.

1. Stand straight with your head erect, chin in, looking straight ahead. Gently turn the head from side to side. Try and look over each shoulder. Turn left, then turn right. Turn left and right again. Only do it as many times as is comfortable. You may feel the neck creaking - a sign it is getting stiff! Take a deep breath, exhaling with a sigh.

2. Stand straight with your head erect, chin in. Lower the head gently to the right shoulder. Now raise it slowly and continue to lower it to the left shoulder. Lower and raise the head several times from side to side. Again do only what is comfortable.

Breathe deeply. Hold it. Exhale with a sigh.

3. Head straight, nicely balanced, chin in. Now drop the head forward and feel the back of the neck stretch. Lift your head slowly. Again only do it as many times as is comfortable.

Do not get over-enthusiastic at the beginning, but build up the number of these exercises over a period of time.

Take three deep breaths.

(2) **Hand and arm exercises**

Let your arms hang loosely by your side, lightly shake your hands, fingers apart, with limp wrists - as the Olympic swimmers do. Gradually let the movement involve your lower arms and elbows, feel them become loose and free. Now shake the entire arm - involve the shoulders - swing them loosely around. You're shaking out all the tension. Do it for a minute to start with.

Take a full deep breath, exhale with a sigh and be aware of the tingling sensations and warmth of the hands.

Take three deep breaths.

(3) **Leg exercises**

Balance yourself by holding on to a chair for stability. Lift your right leg and rotate your foot and ankle, then reverse the rotation. Start shaking your foot, lower leg and knee. Shake it slowly, gradually increase the momentum. Involve your entire leg, shaking the upper thigh. Swing the leg loosely, shaking tension out of the foot, ankle, calf, knee, and thigh. Now exercise the left leg.

Sit down after this exercise and you will feel a tingling, relaxed sensation spread through the legs and feet. You may find it a little difficult at first, so start the exercises gradually. With practice it becomes easy. These exercises are worth doing at any time of the day.

Relaxation

The relaxation sessions should be done in a sitting position - lying down may cause you to fall asleep! During Accelerated Learning periods you must be relaxed but alert.

In an upright chair

Find the position most comfortable for you. Your back should be well supported with your feet flat on the floor one foot apart. The angle of the knees should be slightly more than 90°, i.e. slightly forward from upright. Sit up straight and stretch your spine and neck. Your arms should be hanging straight down at the side of your body. Drop your shoulders and neck and head (almost slump down), place your arms on your thighs, hands towards your knees with your fingers apart. Find the most comfortable position that gives a good balance.

In an armchair

This is similar to the upright chair position. The position of the feet will be the same. Your arms and hands can either rest on the chair arms or your knees, whichever is the most comfortable. Sit well back so your back is supported with your head resting against the chairback in an upright position. Place a cushion against your neck, if the chair back is not high enough to support you.

Sitting on the floor

For those who like to sit on the floor, sit with your back supported against a wall with a cushion in the small of your back. Place your feet 12" apart, turned outwards with your arms on your thighs.

The best place

When you start Awareness Relaxation, you need a place free from interruption and as quiet as possible. Try and be warm, as your body temperature falls slightly during deep relaxation. (If necessary wrap a blanket around yourself). You will find that, after practicing your technique, you can go into a satisfying state of relaxation in a very few minutes. Then a slight noise and disturbance will not bother you. Indeed we find that by using headphones or walkman type personal tape recorders it is possible to practice Accelerated Learning exercises in public places.

Mental relaxation

We have been reviewing exercises that can bring you a wonderful sense of physical relaxation. Creation of full mental relaxation needs a rather more sophisticated technique and this is included on a four part audio-cassette tape, "Introduction to Accelerated Learning" that has been prepared for readers to experience the whole technique.

This tape uses the new concept of Awareness Relaxation. The previous physical exercises have enabled you gradually to become aware of your body's muscles. The mind calming exercises of Awareness Relaxation teach you to produce the same feeling of relaxation by visualisation alone. Just as your mouth watered when you imagined a lemon, you can smooth away stress and attain a refreshing sense of physical and mental relaxation through sheer imagery!

Being able to relax and visualise things "in your mind's eye" is a gift that will not only reduce stress in your life, but will greatly help in achieving the goal of Accelerated Learning. It involves the whole brain, it allows you to reach an Alpha brain wave pattern at will, and it greatly improves your ability to remember through associative imagery.

The tape starts with a simple meditative technique designed to be especially effective, even with people who have never tried any specific form of mind calming exercises before. You quite simply light a candle. This should ideally be in a slightly darkened room irrespective of the time of day. Placed about three feet away, the candle's orange flame is warm and steady. You focus your attention on the flame whilst specially edited baroque music plays. The flame is soothing to look at. This uncomplicated action is nevertheless an important aid in developing your ability to concentrate. While your attention is focussed you attain what Wordsworth called "a happy stillness of mind".

The actual use of the candle is only needed to help your concentration and visualisation for the first few days. Later, after practice, you will be able to see the bright magic of the candle flame in your mind's eye by simply closing your eyes and fixing your gaze at a point in the centre of your forehead.

After the meditative exercise with the candle flame, which you will find beautifully refreshing and relaxing, the tape stimulates your visualisation ability by taking you on an imaginary journey through peaceful country scenes. In the background is a baroque music score and this, with additional evocative and relaxing sound effects, helps to synchronise all your body rhythms - heart, breathing, brain. Not only will your ability to memorise increase but many people report a marked general improvement in their health and emotional life. An indirect bonus that can be equal to the benefit of Accelerated Learning itself.

Many doctors now believe that if we can approach a heart rate of 60 beats a minute our whole bodies and minds work more efficiently - the holistic benefit of mind and body in harmony.

Significantly, when people are performing extraordinary mental feats - superfast mental arithmetic for example - EEG tests show that their bodies are relaxed and that their dominant brain waves are Alpha - 7-13 cycles per second. That's the relaxed and receptive state of mind that the taped exercises achieve.

After a few days practice you will be able to reach an immediate relaxed state at will. Thereafter you can use a simple two minute exercise.

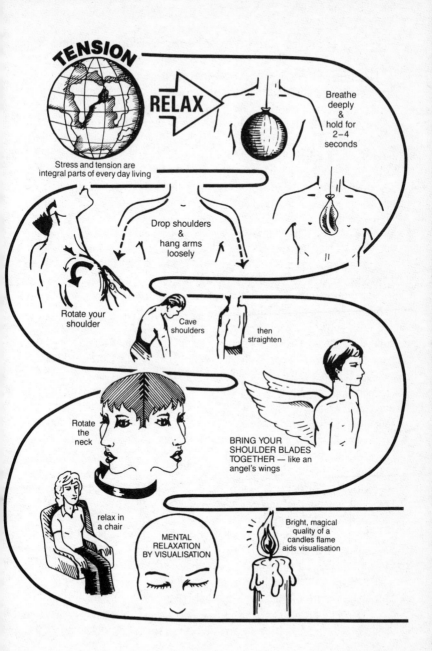

TENSION

RELAX

Breathe deeply & hold for 2–4 seconds

Stress and tension are integral parts of every day living

Drop shoulders & hang arms loosely

Rotate your shoulder

Cave shoulders

then straighten

Rotate the neck

BRING YOUR SHOULDER BLADES TOGETHER — like an angel's wings

relax in a chair

MENTAL RELAXATION BY VISUALISATION

Bright, magical quality of a candles flame aids visualisation

AN ACCELERATED LEARNING COURSE

The following is an exact description of how we have created an Accelerated Learning Language Course. If you follow the technique you can create your own course for your own learning needs.

The pre-recorded Accelerated Language Courses (they are in French, Spanish, Italian, German and English as a Foreign Language) incorporate all the principles we have learnt from our study. They build on the Lozanov techniques by incorporating powerful visualisation aids and by including activities that reflect the three main learning styles. Each is written by a leading language course designer.

An Accelerated Learning Course is designed to transform your ability to learn. You will learn faster, you will learn more easily and you will learn better.

This is clearly a very bold statement to make. However the claim does not have to be taken on trust. We have prepared a Learn-to-Learn double cassette tape and booklet that teaches you how to apply Accelerated Learning to subjects of your own choice.

The double tape has four sides:—

Side 1. Contains a full 30 minutes of specially edited Baroque music. *

Side 2. Contains the relaxation exercises and training in visualisation that really is a delight to experience.

Sides 3. & 4. contain a *full* language lesson (French, Spanish or German).

In conjunction with the lesson text, in the accompanying booklet, these tapes allow you to prove to yourself that you really can learn to recognise the meaning of 300-400 words of a new foreign language in a day! (That's about 15%-20% of a working vocabulary.) You can personally experience the Active and Receptive Baroque music concerts, the power of the memory maps and the effectiveness of the peripheral learning techniques. They also give you a practical example of how to create your own Accelerated Learning Course.

* Excerpts include: Handel Concerto Op. 4 No. 5 and 6, Op. 3 No. 2 and 5; VIVALDI 'Four Seasons'; Albinoni D Minor Op. 9; Pachelbel Kanon L D; Bach Suite 3.

So with the proviso that you can prove, it all for yourself by using the Learn-to-Learn Cassette tapes — here is the full Accelerated Learning technique.

To maximise memory - maximise associations

Accelerated Learning uses a whole range of psychological techniques, to present new material in such a way as to create a number of powerful associations.

Put simply the more associations and the stronger they are, the easier it is to remember and learn.

Our initial courses are for language learning because it is clear that, if Accelerated Learning works well in teaching a foreign language, it will work even faster when you come to learn anything in your native language. For two obvious reasons.

Firstly, when you are learning new material in your own language, it is much easier to form ready associations.

Secondly, it is normally enough to learn the sense of new material. You don't for example have to remember *the exact* form of words printed in your history book, but you *do* have to remember the exact words of a foreign language. Close approximations will not do. (The main exception is learning a play part, which is why the techniques in Accelerated Learning are of especial interest to actors.)

An Accelerated Learning Course is in two parts. Part One is designed to create the basic memory. To get all the vocabulary *into* your head in a relaxed and easy manner. Part Two is designed to let you recall that vocabulary *from* your memory whenever you need it. We have seen that the two tasks are not the same.

In the full description that follows, some of the reasons for each step are repeated, since many readers will use this section as an aide memoire in creating their own courses. You will find that Chapter 14, Accelerated Learning for children, also has important practical hints on developing your own course.

AN ACCELERATED LEARNING LESSON - PART ONE
Step one - Relax

At the beginning of each lesson you carry out a short (2 mins) relaxation and breathing exercise. This calms your mind and creates a relaxed body but receptive mind. It also increases the oxygen supply to the brain which improves brain function. Tension inhibits memory and learning, so you need to get rid of it. The very beginning of each tape has, a very short Baroque music introduction - acting like a 'theme tune' to trigger a mood relaxed receptivity.

Step Two - Context

Each lesson is in the form of a story that takes place in real life and believable, practical situations. You first read through that story in English and the cassette tape tells you the most important new points to notice in your new language. This creates a pleasant sense of security because you know what to expect, and you will fully understand the *context* of the story. You can see that your knowledge of the new language will progress on a well planned smooth route and you know what to look for.

When you prepare an Accelerated Learning Course on the subject in your own language, you should review all the material you want to learn, and then make a note of the central or core ideas. The detail will then become easily associated with those core ideas. When you recall the core ideas, your memory for the subsidiary points is triggered. This economises the number of initial points you have to commit to memory.

This natural mapping principle is instinctive. When you visit a new country or city you look for the landmarks - and then relate other places to them. It is also how we do jigsaws. Doing a jigsaw without the overall picture to guide you is much more difficult.

Step Three - Peripheral Text

The text of the foreign language and the English translation are printed in *two columns side by side on the page* thus -

Philip looks at the house.	**Philip regarde la maison.**
It is big and beautiful.	**Elle est grande et belle.**
Philip goes up to the front door	**Philip s'approche de la porte d'entrée.**
He rings the bell and waits.	**Il sonne et attend.**
An old lady opens the door.	**Une dame âgée ouvre la porte.**
"What do you want young man?" she says.	**"Qu'est-ce que vous voulez jeune homme?" dit-elle.**

The length of the sentences/lines is rarely longer than 7 words. This layout and "chunking" achieves three objectives.

Although your eye may be focussed on the English text, your peripheral vision is taking in the foreign translation and vice versa. So you are already involving your subconscious and are beginning to create some memory - with no conscious effort at all.

Secondly, as we have discovered, the optimum number of bits or "chunks" of new information is about 7.

Thirdly, the fact that the translation is always instantly available means you never have to worry about it. A central principle of Accelerated Learning is that you always feel secure.

Step Four - Make a "mental movie" of the text

You listen to the text of your course for the first time. It is recorded like an Act from a Radio play.

The voices and sound effects create a memorable, dramatic, impression and enable you to visualise in your mind's eye what is happening. Later on you will be able to recall the language by re-running what amounts to a "mental movie" of the language in association with the scenes of the story.

Step Five - More Security

The second reading involves a whispered English translation *first,* followed by the translation text in your new foreign language.

This unusual sequence gives you the maximum confidence and security because you already know the meaning of the new words before you hear them. So you are not tense and consequently you learn quicker. Moreover, the whispered translation subconsciously suggests the text is important and encourages you to use your ear as well as your eye. We have already managed to involve two senses.

Television advertising experts have long known that synchronising the visual picture on the screen, plus the voice over, (plus ideally a supertitle to "drive the point home") is the best way to create memory. The advertiser has only a few seconds in which to make you remember; we use the same technique but you can replay the tape as often as you want.

Step Six - Visual Associations to Add Right Brain Power

After two readings on the cassette tape you will now be ready to use our powerful and unique language memory maps.

Remember, how we emphasised that when you find your way around a new town you look for the landmarks? Well, a memory map takes the main words and concepts you want to remember and links them, together with lines and pictures.

A memory map is a good representation of how the brain actually works. The brain does *not* work in neat linear logic going steadily from A to B, B to C, and so on. Left to right conventional printing on a page is, therefore, not necessarily "natural". It is merely a useful but contrived way of organising information. Teachers of young children will confirm that when they begin to learn to read they will often read left to right and then want to drop a line and read the next line from right to left - thus:

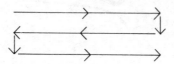

Moreover, a large body of Middle Eastern and Far Eastern languages are read from right to left.

The Language Memory Map is a unique way of pictorialising the lesson, putting text into a visual form. Since pictures are remembered far better than spoken words, and since the right brain is now brought into action, memory maps have a double benefit. They produce powerful visual images and they stimulate right brain activity.

The whole brain, left and right working in harmony, will be constantly creating and recalling associations and making connections. Moreover, the whole brain can take in information from many different sources simultaneously. Look at the memory map below. See how the chunked text on the page above has been transferred to a memory map. See how the words are written on connecting lines or are lettered over, or associated with, pictures.

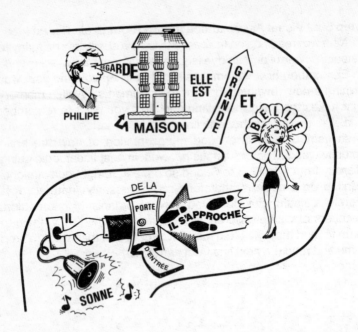

The memory map is a very, very powerful teaching aid in Accelerated Learning. Partly because it presents the material in a way that is natural to the brain and partly because it creates a very strong visual image. So now you are creating a series of easily remembered *visual associations* for your new vocabulary.

In Step Six you turn on your tape recorder and listen to the text spoken in a soft, confidential tone, while you follow the text on your Memory Map. Not all the simpler words are included but the ideas are linked together in groups. The idea is to enable you to fix the language in your mind's eye. To associate words with pictures.

On Side 2 of the Introductory tape we include training in visualisation. If you can get the language lesson successfully visualised "in your mind's eye", you will create a semi-photographic memory for it, and your learning will become astonishingly easy.

By the end of Step Six you will have made significant progress in the process of creating strong associations for your new vocabulary.

Step Seven - Sound Associations to Add Right Brain Power

Next comes the "Active Concert". In this step you will again be listening to the text. Now, however, it is spoken over a background of Baroque music. Baroque music, which is at 60 beats to the minute, is very relaxing, calms the mind, increases the proportion of Alpha brain waves and stimulates right brain activity.

Because the voice is used, almost like an instrument in the orchestra, "sound surfing" over the music, we are creating a strong sound association with the new vocabulary that you're learning.

The text becomes better fixed in your memory, and we have now introduced yet another memory aid - rhythm. The lesson can become as easy as learning a song.

Because the music is mainly processed by the right brain, whereas speech is a left brain activity, you are helping to synchronise left and right brain activity. Two brains are not only better than one, they promote faster learning!

Step Eight - Relax Again

Take a two minute break to repeat the simple breathing and relaxing exercises. You are now prepared for even deeper relaxation.

Step Nine - Let Your Subconscious do the Work

Now you will be coming to the end of Part One of your first lesson.

Close your book and turn on the tape recorder. Relax and shut your eyes. You will now listen to a second Baroque music concert. This time the music is the dominant sound - and the text of your lesson is being spoken at a low (but audible) level. The music again appeals to your right brain and creates a receptive, relaxed mood. Now, however, the words are intended to be directly addressed to your subconscious. The new language in a real sense is being "floated" quietly and gently into your mind.

The end of the second, or passive, Baroque concert concludes Part One, of each lesson. The whole sequence takes about 45 minutes. In that short time:-

1) You will have learned to recognise about 300 words in real life

193

practical sentences. (Any language expert will confirm that that is an astonishing achievement.)

2) The grammar has largely been subconsciously absorbed.
3) You've created a whole series of strong associations in your mind - both visual and sound.
4) You've been relaxed, so you'll feel fresh at the end.
5) You've synchronised left and right brain activity.
6) You've been using your peripheral vision and,
7) You've involved your subconscious as well as your conscious, your limbic system as well as your new brain.

In other words you will have succeeded in co-ordinating all the elements that go to achieve successful (Accelerated) Learning.

But there's still more!

Part One of the lesson is designed to create a deep and accurate memory of your new language. It has been largely passive learning however.

Ideally you will now stop and not start Part Two until the following day. This is to let the new information "sink in", since we believe that your brain uses part of sleep as a way to rehearse and store new information.

AN ACCELERATED LEARNING LESSON - PART TWO
Active Recall on Demand

Next day you start Part Two of your lesson. This involves a whole series of interesting and enjoyable activities that involve you directly with the new vocabulary you have learnt.

We learn best when we are personally involved, so this part is all active participation, games, etc. It looks like fun, but again we use simple techniques that have been found to be highly effective in transforming the recognition you have undoubtedly achieved for your new language, into the ability to recall that vocabulary on demand and use it fluently in practical and different situations.

The "Activation" exercises you follow in Part Two of each language lesson, has scope for all three styles or "modes" of learning - Auditory, Visual and Kinaesthetic. Again the techniques are described in relation to our pre-recorded Accelerated Learning Courses, but the principles can be used and adapted if you are preparing your own Accelerated Learning course, whatever the subject.

Step One - Relax

Follow through the simple 2 minute breathing and relaxation exercises. This is calming and also provides you with an ideal mental "set" or attitude for learning.

Step Two - Warm Up

The soft confidential reading is repeated again (Step Six of Part One). Follow the Memory Map.

This provides a review and a warm-up for learning. No athlete would dream of simply going out onto the track and trying to perform at peak efficiency. They always "warm-up". So should a peak performance learner.

Step Three - Involve Yourself

Use a series of coloured pencils to highlight, underline, or mark up any words in the Memory Map that are important to you. It actively involves you and your personal contribution helps fix the material in your mind's eye. (This is a visual and kinaesthetic exercise.)

Step Four - Train your Ear

We next provide a "pronunciation period". It lets you listen to how sounds are pronounced in the foreign language. It's vital to get the pronunciation right early on, because researchers have found that we tend to repeat our earliest attempts at foreign language pronunciation - so if its right at the beginning it will always be right. If its wrong you have to unlearn it later.

Every language has its own "music", rhythm and intonation. Indeed every language has a characteristic frequency. Babies learn to react to this frequency in the womb. So your own language is literally inborn in you. We have developed exercises in the cassette, and visuals in the book, to help you develop an "ear" for the cadences of the language straight away.

You'll listen to the cassette and repeat some key phrases. You are also now starting to treat your tape recorder as your partner. This is important, because you need to bring your new language actively alive. Since most pre-recorded courses are used by yourself, the more interaction we can achieve with this tape the better.

Step Five - Involve yourself in Realistic Dialogue

Next you will find the vocabulary you've already learned put into *dialogue* form. Often in the form of questions and answers between two characters. You thus become used to normal conversations. You can become actively involved in these dialogues by repeating the words and by playing the part of one of the characters. You can, for example, answer before your character does, by pressing the pause button on your cassette player.

Step Six - Involve yourself in personalised dialogue

Now follows what we call *personalised* dialogues. In this step you are asked questions directly and you must answer for your own personal circumstances - name, nationality etc. Again you are treating your tape recorder as a partner and the language comes alive and relevant to you personally. We encourage you to walk around, gesticulate and act out the answers. It is a dress rehearsal for real life situations and is again active involvement in which you use as many of the senses as possible.

Step Seven - Take a Break

Take a short break. In a learning situation we remember best what was at the beginning and the end of the session. Concentration (and memory) wanes in the middle so the shorter the middle, the better the learning.

Step Eight - Maximum Communication with Minimum Effort

Next step involves another unique idea built into Accelerated Learning Language courses. We call it "learning the Multiplier Words and Phrases".

A multiplier phrase, (or word) is one that doesn't take much effort to learn, but once learnt, generates a huge amount of practical language use. Thus, if you simply learn the French for "What is that called - give me one please." you would be able to go shopping in France for almost anything.

There are "multiplier" words and phrases in every lesson. They also illustrate a simple, but important, principle. The principle of the most communication for least memory.

Moreover, if you learn a lot of *usable* vocabulary quickly, you rapidly gain confidence and enjoyment in your new ability. It's the joy of learning in a practical form.

Step Nine - Rhyme and Reason

In each language lesson we provide "grammar jingles". Whilst a lot of grammar is unconsciously absorbed from the lesson itself, there are obviously rules you simply must know to speed up your learning. So we have put the grammar rules in rhyme form, or sometimes even in a chant or song form.

Learning the number of days in the month is easy to remember because of the rhyme:

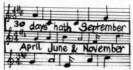

The information has been "chunked" into short sentences and secondly, it has rhythm and rhyme. In the same way grammar points are easy and pleasant to learn if they are expressed in rhythm and rhyme. So we do.

Step Ten - Visualise the Language

This step is of great importance. It will appear simple but its effect is powerful. You sit quietly and close your eyes. Then, with a blank tape in your tape recorder, you visualise the entire scene you have been learning in Part One *and describe it out loud* in your new language. You can either use the verbatim words, if you remember them so perfectly, or just use what words you can remember. Don't necessarily try to make proper sentences, it is too early. Just use the nouns, adjectives or verbs that come into your mind as you visualise the scenes.

Step Eleven - Become as a Child

The lesson ends with some fun games

* There's a word square game to complete in your text book.
* There's some true or false questions.
* In each lesson there's a different game to play that indirectly teaches you something (e.g. numbers or colours) without you even realising it).

In the Language text book we provide another, simple idea, which is a fun way to boost your learning effortlessly.

Each Course contains a set of word cards. These cards contain most of the verbs, nouns and adjectives that have already been learnt.

In French, for example, masculine nouns are printed blue, feminine nouns are printed pink. The adjectives are printed in both the feminine and masculine versions. The top half of an adjective card is masculine and printed blue, the bottom half is feminine and printed pink. This automatically teaches the learner to match up the correct masculine or feminine ending as appropriate to the noun.

Example -

La maison / Une maison	Pink
Le lit / Un lit	Blue
Grand	Blue
Grande	Pink

The word cards enable a great deal of interesting, involved and peripheral learning to take place.

Firstly they can be used to build up sentences from words you have already learnt, but in quite new ways. Or the learner can sort the cards out into nouns, verbs, adjectives and prepositions (remember Tulving's success?). Then take three cards from each pile and try to make up a sentence using as many of the cards as possible.

Or use the cards as "flash cards" to rehearse the meanings in a moment of spare time, e.g. on a train journey.

Or take the word cards for objects commonly found around the house. By fixing the word in your new language for "door" actually on the door, or "lamp" on the lamp, you have an automatic and largely subconscious prompt every time you pass by. It's an effortless way to absorb vocabulary.

There's an important point of principle throughout Step Two. Almost all the learning is in the form of *games*, in which you are actively involved. The nearer you can get to the open receptivity of a child, the faster you will learn.

"Become as a child" and you really will become a highly successful Accelerated Learner.

The Name Game

A unique feature of the Accelerated Learning Language Courses is a section called **The Name Game.** This is based on the fact that English and other European foreign languages have a common origin. Over hundreds of years they have evolved to look and sound different - but the difference can be likened to extreme dialects of the same languages. Once you see how this evolution has taken place, it is easy and fun to appreciate, at a glance, the meanings of thousands of Spanish, French or German words.

A simple illustration proves the point. Over the years z in German has often evolved into a 't' sound in English, thus **zoll** = 'toll' or duty, **zinn** = 'tin' and **zu** = 'to'.

Similarly, the vowel sound **ei** in German is now often represented by 'o' in English, so **stein** = 'stone' and **allein** = 'alone'.

Knowing the above it is easy to work out why **zwei** = 'two' in English, why **malz** is 'malt' and **bein** is 'bone'.

The Name Game is a good example of how involvement and the creation of associations make learning faster and more enjoyable.

Learning Versus Acquisition

Our Accelerated Learning Method as applied to languages has much in common with the principles expounded by Stephen Krashen and Tracy Terrell in their recent and influential book "The Natural Approach".

They point out the total failure for most people of the grammar based methods of language teaching. This approach, is still unfortunately the "norm" in schools, even though almost everyone finds it boring and the poor results are all too evident.

The simple truth is that the goal of the grammar and drill based lessons is different from what people in the real world want. Most people learn a language in order to communicate.

To communicate you need to know enough vocabulary in order to express ideas, wants and opinions and describe the world about you. Grammar is only the framework for that expression and *by definition is secondary to vocabulary.*

As anyone knows, who has learned a foreign language by "picking it up" in the country itself, communicative ability is acquired really quite rapidly, easily and enjoyably - grammatical accuracy on the other hand increases much more slowly - after experience of actually using the language.

As Krashen puts it so well, grammar is a model, a "monitor" you eventually come to have in your head, which tells you instinctively whether, what you have just said "sounds" or "feels" right. But that, by definition, pre-supposes that the production of words to communicate comes first, and the use of grammar as a monitor, comes second.

States Krashen *'The mistake is to assume that a conscious understanding of grammar is a pre-requisite to acquiring communicative competence.*

'Early exposure of the systematic organization of the grammatical form of the language is neither necessary nor sufficient for the learners mastery of the language. Presentation of particular instances of language in contexts which exemplify their meaning and use is both sufficient and necessary.'

In other words, understanding the meaning of what is said to you in a natural context is the first priority. In this way you *acquire* language. Afterwards comes *learning* the rules or grammar.

This distinction between acquisition and learning may sound slight but in fact it is highly significant. Every one of us *acquires* our own native language, and we do it easily and effortlessly. Only later do we *learn* the formal rules of grammar.

The emphasis of our Accelerated Learning Language Courses

is on acquiring language for practical communication.

Only when the use of language becomes an unconscious skill do we become fluent. Clearly if, before we said something, we had to:-

* Rehearse the sentence in our mind,
* "Monitor" whether the structure was correct,
* Know the "rules" involved in that structure,
- then we would talk falteringly, if at all! In natural speech we concentrate on what is being said, not how it is being said.

Yet conventional foreign language teaching is concerned far too much with how things are said. It is concerned with learning rather than acquisition. Concentration on language learning and making continuous corrections, leads to hesitancy, lack of confidence, a diminishing of your natural fluency. Learning is a conscious process, whereas acquisition is a sub-conscious process and, therefore, much easier.

We are not saying that you do not need grammar - clearly you do. But learning grammar comes naturally and easily after you have acquired a reasonable vocabulary and communicative ability.

If this natural sequence is followed then grammar no longer becomes a tedious and off-putting chore. It becomes a source of pleasure and pride, because you have the feeling of putting some elegance and sophistication to your new language.

How Best to Acquire a Language

Acquisition of language takes place quite simply and automatically when you understand what you are reading or listening to.

This is why we stress the use of "peripheral prompt" translations in Accelerated Learning, and the Memory Maps that tie together words and pictures. We acquire when we focus our attention on what is being said, and we acquire when we are confident.

One source of that confidence, is the knowledge that it takes time to be able to speak in your new target language. An infant understands far more than she can initially say, and speaks when she is ready.

So you must expect the initial spoken words in your new language to be flawed and inaccurate - just as the infants is. This, however, is just a natural phase and will automatically be superceded by increased fluency.

Since your ability to understand will initially outstrip your ability to speak, there is simply no need to speak much before you are ready. Expect too that your early steps in speaking will be to answer with one or two word answers, then simple phrases, and only later with sentences.

If you approach the learning of a language with a relaxed attitude, you'll succeed just as well as you did when you learned your own language.

It is the way that the Accelerated Learning Language Courses have been prepared. The grammar has been *embedded* in the course and you'll acquire the rules implicitly, just as you learned your own language. Naturally there are also explicit grammar explanations, because as an adult you can accept and understand rules much faster than an infant. Moreover since the Accelerated Learning Course teaches you a large proportion of the basic language in such a short time, the "naturally good learner" will instinctively want the grammar rules to provide a structure. But the grammar explanation never gets in the way of meaning and communication.

If we envisage grammar based / left brain emphasis learning to be at one end of the spectrum and meaningful input / right brain emphasis acquisition to be at the other end, then an Accelerated Learning Course lies towards the "right" (see figure) However, because the grammar rules are clearly provided, everyone whether "acquirer" or "learner", can progress in whichever way they feel most comfortable.

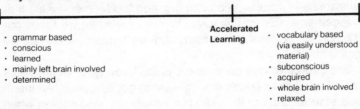

	Accelerated Learning	
· grammar based		· vocabulary based (via easily understood material)
· conscious		· subconscious
· learned		· acquired
· mainly left brain involved		· whole brain involved
· determined		· relaxed

Creating your own Course

Let us now consider how you might create an Accelerated Learning Courses of your own for two different subjects.

1) French homework for a lesson from a conventional school course

   or

2) Learning a new scientific technique. For example memorising the elements in Accelerated Learning itself!

Example One - The French Homework

Here is a quick check list of what you might do.

1) You would certainly do 2 minutes breathing and relaxing.

2) You would write the vocabulary out in side by side columns and/or you'd "chunk" the text if that was appropriate.

3) You'd record the material to learn on your tape recorder with appropriate baroque music playing in the background on a second tape recorder or music centre.

4) You would sketch out a quick memory map - it only takes a few minutes. You'd connect the words and phrases that had associations.

5) You would play back your own recording (with the Baroque music now automatically in the background). And you would follow it on your side by side text.

   This does pre-suppose you have access to two tape recorders (or a tape recorder & music centre). However, we find most people do, or can borrow an extra tape recorder.

6) You would underline the important words in a coloured pen or highlighter pen (visual involvement).

7) You would walk around and act out the words (active or kinaesthetic involvement).

8) You would close your eyes and try to make up a story, *however* simple, using the words you have learnt and visualising the scenes in your minds' eye.

9) You would perhaps make up some "flash" cards and play some of the word games.

What we promise you, is that the little extra work and time you put in at this stage, will be repaid manifold by the fact that your learning will be much faster and more thorough than using conventional methods. Do a little more work now, and save a *lot* of work later.

A short anecdote would be appropriate here. As the techniques of Accelerated Learning were being discussed in our office one of our colleagues rather hesitantly asked whether it would work for her 9 year old daughter, Rachel? *'Absolutely, it would'* we said. We made a visit and taught her just two elements. How to record her homework over the Baroque music and how to write down the words on a side by side list. Then we told her to play your tape half an hour before going to bed and again in the morning, (she has a Walkman type machine).

Coincidently there was a parents evening two weeks later. The French teacher button-holed our colleague and asked, *'What on earth have you done with Rachel? She's been transformed. Her marks are near perfect, and she's gone from 22nd in class to 3rd in class in two weeks!'* We believe strongly that just as a vicious circle is all too easily created, where a few poor results create a long term negative attitude and expectations of failure - so Accelerated Learning has proved over and over again that you can create a "virtuous circle" where success breeds success. You break out of the vicious circle and create instead a positive expectation of accomplishment.

The virtuous circle is a major benefit of the Accelerated Learning technique.

Example Two - Remembering the elements in a pre-recorded Accelerated Learning French Course.

Let's suppose the concept of Accelerated Learning was completely new to you. You would:-
a) Do 2 minutes breathing and relaxing exercises.
b) Read through the description. You have already done that in Chapter 13.
c) You would pull out the core ideas and maybe highlight them. The list on the opposite page is a fair summary.
d) You would create a memory map. Make sure the key words on the memory map trigger a lot of associations (usually you use concrete nouns and verbs). You would draw some simple

pictures as that helps.

Try to use words or connections that produce strong images. Use connecting lines so the ideas would branch out, in the way that the brain makes connections. Print so the visual image is strong.

Maybe the memory maps would look like those on the following page.

e) Record the words on the memory map on one tape recorder with the Baroque music playing in the background (using a 2nd) tape recorder).

f) Play it back and follow your memory map, thereby fixing it in both your auditory and visual memory.

g) Close your eyes and follow the memory map in your mind's eye, describing the sequence of events out loud. Thereby synchronising left and right brains.

An Accelerated Learning Language Course
A Summary of the core ideas and sequence of steps

Part I - Creating the Memory

a) 300-400 words per 45 minute lesson.

b) Powerful association is key to memory.

c) The strongest associations involve right brain and link it to left brain (i.e. pictures & words or music & words or pictures & words & music).

Steps are:-

1) Relax, deep breath.

2) Establish the context of lesson in English. A jigsaw picture gives security.

3) Review side by side text in "chunked" sentences.

4) Play 1st lesson. Female voice is reassuring.

5) Play 2nd version. Whispered English translation comes first. Since you already know meaning, you can concentrate on the new language without tension. More security.

6) Review memory map. Reproduces way brain works. Turns lesson into a *pictorial* form. Visual memory is strongest type of memory. Also visualisation is a mainly right brain activity. So a memory map creates strong visual association to speed the

creation of memory **and** provokes right brain activity in synchronised support of left brain learning.

7) Listen to Active Concert. Text is spoken over a background of Baroque music. Now it is the music that provokes right brain activity. The music is relaxing and also creates an emotive and sound association for the new vocabulary. Rhythm helps too. Pop song example.

8) Relax - deep breath.

9) Allow passive concert to float vocabulary directly into sub-consciousness.

The above sequence creates a unique presentation which achieves peripheral learning, left/right brain involvement and conscious/subconscious learning.

10) Overnight break to let material "sink in".

Part II - Turning recognition into recall through activation

a) We remember best what we're actively involved in.

b) All three learning modes need expression - visual, auditory and kinaesthetic (Modes V, A and K).

c) Indirect learning is often best - through games. Become as a child is the key.

Steps are:-

1) Relax, deep breath.

2) Highlight, colour, underline memory map. Involves. (Mode V and K)

3) Listen to lesson and review Memory Map - Provides Warm Up.

4) Practice Pronunciation Period - creates an 'ear' for the language (Mode A)

5) Act out dialogues on tape. Active involvement (Mode A and K)

6) Personalise the dialogues. Provide relevant and active involvement (Mode A and K)

7) Take a Break. Improves memory.

8) Learn multiplier phrases. Maximum communication/minimum effort.

9) Learn grammar jingles. Chants and rhymes are easily recalled.

10) Visualise scene of lesson. Speak it out loud, synchronise Right and Left brain.

11) Play the games - puzzles, word cards, flash cards. Indirect stress free learning through *active* pleasurable involvement (Modes V and K).

Summary

90 minutes of tape time - 300/400 words in two days - finish relaxed and refreshed.

Part I

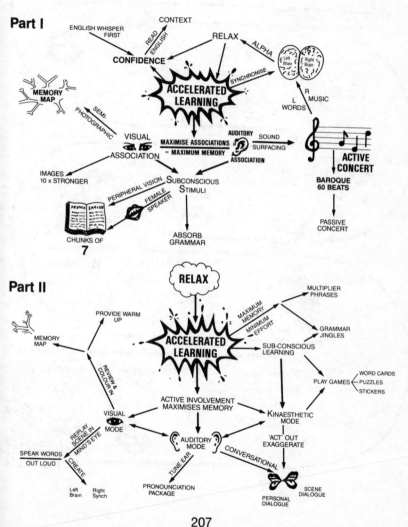

Part II

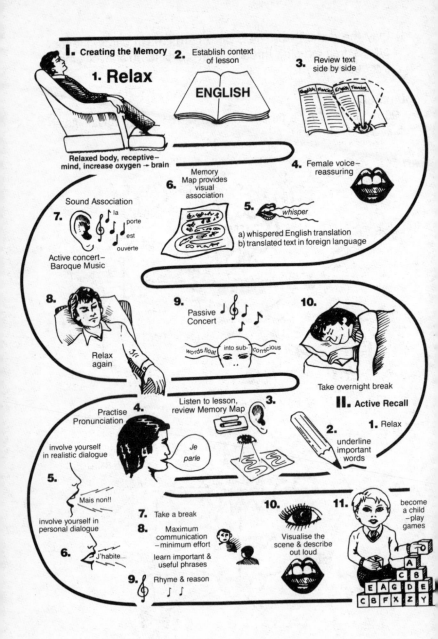

208

ACCELERATED LEARNING FOR YOUR CHILDREN

The importance of a rich environment in the pre-school period cannot be overstressed.

In conjunction with three leading universities we are now preparing a whole programme for the pre-school child. Teaching them good principles of learning, plus spelling and reading in a relaxed and fun manner, it will also provide a stimulating environment, an appreciation of music and the basis of an enquiring mind.

Meanwhile the following points will be useful for parents working with older children already at school.

As a preamble we cannot do better than quote Glenn Doman, a leading if controversial educationalist in America.

'The brain,' he says, *'has infinite capacity. The more you put in the more it will hold. The human brain grows by use - the way biceps do. Everytime we use visualisation, the ability to visualise expands.'*

On TV Glenn Doman showed how a child's latent abilities can be 'schooled out'.

When he held up cards with dots on them, pre-school children could tell the number without making an individual count. Yet after 3 years of teaching these children to count using a linear approach, they had lost the right brain ability for instant instinctual arithmetic.

Doman believes passionately in the role of the parent in providing lots of learning to small children at normal speeds. He argues that if you slow everything down, you are implying the child cannot learn faster. The child adjusts his rate of learning downwards, to match your (low) expectations. Its a vicious circle, that all too often leads to the unwitting constriction of latent ability.

Expect a lot from your child and she or he will achieve a lot. Children can memorise more information than most adults - which is why our language courses use so many activities that recreate a

, child-like receptivity.

Are Women the best Teachers?

Mothers, are probably the world's best teachers. With no formal training - perhaps because of no formal training - they oversee the most dramatic learning period in every human's life.

Instinctively the mother creates an ideal learning climate. It is loving, supportive, positive. For the child there is an emotional context to each new situation.

Her gestures and tone are encouraging. She praises success and any mistakes are corrected by showing the *right* way to act, rather than dwelling on the original error. She instinctively develops the child's ability to visualise through stories.

It is a sobering fact that the Coleman Report on Education in U.S.A., concluded that schools have *'little effect on the outcome of a childs education.'* Mark Twain expressed it cynically when he said, *'I never let my schooling interfere with my education.'*

The truth is that the education of children from families in which the thinking of children is respected, in which their creativity is encouraged, in which human values and intellectual values are placed high, is mostly successful and their eventual success in the world is almost inevitable. In families in which children are condemned as little and foolish, patterns of failure are quickly established and minds are wasted.

Good music, good books around the home, art books, pictures and a sense that there is an adventure in acquiring knowledge, will automatically stimulate a desire for learning - and that is half the battle.

Be Positive

Every single comment about your child's learning and ability should be loving, supportive and POSITIVE. We have seen how easily the mind absorbs negative suggestions and how such comments suggest artificial limits on one's ability.

It is vital to suggest that learning will be easy and pleasant and that your child can achieve the results she or he desires. This does not mean you ignore reality - but a poor mark in one test, for example, is just that. It means that a particular piece of information was not well learned - it does not mean the child is "no good" at the subject in general. Individual mistakes are not important. Success will follow if the child is encouraged to think creatively.

Encourage questions

When you answer a question, try not to provide a final answer that discourages further thought - instead leave your child something to reflect on.

Prepare a Mental Map

Work out a summary of what's to be learned. An overview, use key words, phrases and short sentences. You are picking out the core ideas. Make the words and phrases as evocative as possible. Write down words that are easy to visualise in your "mind's eye"

These notes should be written down or typed in large letters so that they can be used later as elaborations. They can be fastened to the wall or in places where they form a constant stimulus to the peripheral vision. The bedroom is ideal. A memory map is the superior form, because it is so visual. Posters are also good because the information is in part subconsciously assimilated. Make the words or pictures as dramatic or funny or bizarre as possible. The core ideas of any subject are not so many. The essentials of arithmetic can be learnt in hours. Remember to "chunk" and to teach your child the way to make a Memory Map.

Taping the Material

Remember to have an Active Concert - and a Passive Concert - for each lesson to be learned. The active concert should involve Baroque music playing in the background while you record the material. As you read the material to be learned, become an Actor. Express the words with emotion, sometimes forcefully. Raise your voice when the music is loud and lower your voice to caress the music when it is soft. Follow the rhythm of the music where you can - but don't concentrate on this to the extent of losing the meaning. Imagine you are a great Shakespearean actor. Art is a powerful means of teaching.

After a little practice you'll find it easy and fun to do and quite normal. Don't be shy or embarrassed. The knowledge of how powerful the technique is, will be your motivation. You can always listen to check back on personal earphones!

When you prepare both the active and passive concerts you can use the specially edited Baroque music available on the Introductory Tapes.

For the passive concert the spoken word is softer and calmer. If possible try and adjust the positioning of the microphones of your tape recorder so that the music is the more dominant sound on the finished tape. This way your child can later play back the passive concert as an enjoyable musical background in the house, kitchen, bathroom or travelling in the car.

It's the easiest, most pleasant way to ensure the material is automatically absorbed.

It will be apparent that the preparation of a do it yourself Accelerated Learning Course requires two tape recorders. Ideally you would use a Walkman style personal tape player, so that the range of play back possibilities is as wide as possible.

Be imaginative with your Activations - the next-day activities that fix the inforrmation in the mind. Most of the good Activations involve games and puzzles. If you build in some of the following activities, you can be actively involved in helping your child in his or her studying.

In language learning, several well known games can be incorporated. Bingo is an excellent way to learn numbers - as are card games such as Pontoon.

"Simon says" can be played with just two people and is a good fun way to learn verbs.

TV quiz games can be adapted to learn adjectives and whole sentences. Playing charades usually engrosses people's attention enough so they talk unselfconsciously in their new language.

You can make up cards, with opposites or synonyms on and then play matching them up. Or you can make up cards with individual words and then use them to form sentences.

A game an older son or daughter can play on their own is to try translating the sense of a news bulletin as its being transmitted. Or they could imagine themselves in a big department store going from department to department ordering things. Or they can describe each room of their house in turn.

Some Practical Hints

Whether you are using a pre-recorded course from Accelerated Learning Systems, or making your own tape for homework, there are a few basic points to remember.

The more you relax the better you learn

The music does an excellent job of relaxing you automatically. But a few days preparatory practice with the relaxation exercise contained on the Introductory tape will prove of immense benefit.

Adult learners might be tempted to think that a glass of wine will also reduce tension and would add to the relaxation! We strongly advise against it. The relaxation exercise and music creates a relaxed alertness and heightened suggestibility. Alcohol will have the opposite effect. It will slow down the process of the brain and reduce the effectiveness with which the material is encoded in your memory.

Enjoy it - or stop!

Every Accelerated Learning Session should be an enjoyable time. 45 minutes to 90 minutes is enough. Once you or your child find interest diminishing, stop for the day. The brain is working less effectively.

Don't be a Puritan

The initial reaction of some older children is that Accelerated Learning can't be working. They are often the ones who do best at school in formal education. That's logical, because they are among the comparatively few who are successful in, and rewarded by, a system where progress equals effort.

So when it all seems effortless, fun and relaxed, their sub-conscious effectly say "This can't work because it's too easy". We now know how devious our subconscious is. It will try to find ways to prove itself right.

Accelerated Learning challenges deeply ingrained thinking, built up over years that says that learning has to be difficult. So learners need to recognise this inhibition for what it is. You will be storing a lot in your long term memory, without fully realising it, and it may take a day or two for you to relax enough to let it out!

Try and Play back on a Walkman Tape machine

These personal playback machines are now relatively cheap and have the great advantage that they enable you to playback your sessions in private at any time, any place.

The stereo effect on the headphones and the fact that the left and right earphones can be separately adjusted for sound also helps.

Passive in the Evening - Active in the Morning!

Bearing in mind the way that your brain files, assimilates and stores information during sleep, it is a good idea to play the passive concert as a background in the late evening.

A review period with the active part of the tape the next morning is ideal - especially for children engaged in a test that day.

Remember to involve A.V. and K.

Your child will learn best if all the learning modes are involved. Work out a procedure where there are auditory, visual and kinaesthetic involvements. If you can establish your child's preferred learning style (see Chapter 10) you can create a learning pattern thats tailor-made for him - with a big boost in his enjoyment and success.

Form a Group

If you, or your child, are learning with a pre-recorded Accelerated Learning course, a good way to extend your knowledge would be to form a small local group. It gives you a chance to try out your new language, to interact together, and read foreign language magazines. You might perhaps take a trip to the nearest restaurant specialising in that nationality's food and order in your new language. Get some foreign language books out of the library.

The Accelerated Learning Association whose address is in the next chapter will give you assistance in forming local groups if you write to them.

HOW YOU CAN BE INVOLVED

Accelerated Learning is evolving quickly into a world-wide movement, embraced not only by individual schools and universities, but by National and State Educational authorities.

We hope this book will excite your interest. The application of the Accelerated Learning method is as broad as you want it to be - for homework, for induction courses, hobbies, re-training, language learning and, of course, for specific subjects - computer programming, English literature, history, geography, mathematics, physics and chemistry. This book has been directed to people who want to take advantages of Accelerated Learning in their home environment, or at least working on their own or in small groups.

We know already of dozens of individuals who are already applying the methods to their own specialist subjects. In doing so they are continually evolving practical improvements and ideas. For them, and we hope for you, we have founded **The Accelerated Learning Association.**

The Association will publish a regular bulletin that describes the latest findings on Accelerated Learning from around the world. It will include articles and will review and list worthwhile literature and books. The Association will invite interested professionals to prepare Accelerated Learning Courses in a wide variety of subjects, and will then edit, layout, print and record those courses. The resulting courses will then be offered for sale to the membership of the Association. The originators will receive a Royalty on world wide sales. In this way the number of subjects given the "Accelerated Learning" treatment will expand rapidly, the income will be returned to the early pioneers, and the movement will have a continuously expanding catalogue of material.

There is a small annual subscription price for membership which includes the bulletins and the address is "Accelerated

Learning Association'', 50 Aylesbury Road, Aston Clinton, Aylesbury, Bucks, ENGLAND. Tel. (0296) 631177.

Those readers who are professional teachers - rather than learners - may also want to join SALT Society for Accelerated Learning and Teaching - whose address is Box No. 1216, Welch Station, Ames, Iowa 50010 U.S.A, or SEAL, Society for Effective Affective Learning, c/o Western Language Centre, Forge House, Kemble, Gloucestershire, GL7 6AD. This society arranges teacher training courses and meetings and publishes a journal.

The Accelerated Learning Association will be pleased to hear of your practical experiences and successes. Letters will be individually answered. The Bulletin will also report on the progress of the pre-school programme currently in preparation.

The Association will be helpful in another way. People who have experienced Accelerated Learning sometimes raise an objection (which is nevertheless a powerful indirect compliment). They ask what to do with the extra time they have. One obvious answer is to do another course! Thus when Don Schuster of Iowa State University taught 1 year of Spanish in 3 months, he spent the extra time in teaching French. Since the effect appears cumulative, it seems a good solution and the Association can keep you informed on all new courses.

In North America readers interested in joining the Accelerated Learning Association or purchasing the Learn-to-Learn tapes or Full Language Courses should contact:—

Accelerated Learning Systems (N.A.) Inc.

3028 Emerson Ave S

Minneapolis

MN 55408

(612) 827 4856

NOTES FOR TEACHERS

Accelerated Learning is easy and effective for the student, precisely because it is more demanding on the teacher. The teacher must learn to present material in ways that are very easily absorbed into the students long term memory.

Leading expert on Accelerated Learning is Charles Schmid of the L I N D Institute, San Francisco. He holds 5 day teacher training programmes all over the world. We asked him to contribute some suggestions as to how a teacher, new to the principles of Accelerated Learning, might start implementing them in a classroom situation.

Accepting that the basic structure of the course would follow the lines already detached for home study, he made the following suggestions that are specific to group teaching.

The Classroom

Students should feel welcomed. If possible have a horseshoe shape arrangement for the chairs. There is then no barrier between teacher and students and the teacher can use his body kinaesthetically. A rug on the floor, and ideally some flowers, is pleasant and music playing as students enter, immediately creates a positive and happy atmosphere. Fade the music down gradually when you are ready - do not cut it off abruptly. A flipchart is preferable to a black board, because you can use colour and you can refer back, whereas once something is erased from a blackboard it is gone forever. A few pictures on the wall, changed regularly, implies that you are creating a fresh environment, something new to look forward to, and that the teacher cares about the students learning.

Tuning Up

Students arrive in class with varying degrees of interest and at varying levels of energy. If you equate these levels, they should be able to absorb the information about equally. Even for adults, throwing a ball around the class works. The 2 minutes breathing exercises are very important. The students need to understand the paradox that relaxation is the ideal state in which to learn. Many initially misunderstand the word relaxation in this context. It is a state of relaxed awareness, rather than relaxation on the way to sleep. If you relax, you liberate energy, and you therefore have more energy with which to learn.

Verbal Suggestion

Choice of words can be important. Words are so easily construed positively or negatively.

For example "DIFFICULT". Something difficult is really only something that requires more practice. It was originally difficult to ride a bike or to swim - but now it is easy.

For example "DON'T". "Don't forget to bring your books tomorrow", has in it a hidden command which is "forget to bring your books". Prefer instead "Bring your books tomorrow" - it is a positive command.

Non-Verbal Suggestion

Voice tone, eye contact, facial expression, all communicate more about your feelings for the subjects than the words. They should communicate enthusiasm. Students should feel free to make mistakes without being put down - because then they will try out new things.

Role Playing

In language classes, it is very useful to have the student take on the identity of someone in his new language. It brings him closer to the culture of specific occupation. Jobs such as wine grower, or baker work well. In non-language areas it can be hugely productive to have students take on the personna of a real person in that field. One physics teacher in a junior High School gave out names of famous scientists - Gallileo, Copernicus, Einstein, Oppenheimer. The students chose one and became that scientist for the term. They researched their life and history and not only reported back to other students in the first person - but had round table discussions. The students' imagination was excited, and they became involved - so they learnt.

In history, it would be good to have some music of the period, and to have the students visualise the action of the period. Queen Elizabeth debating with her ministers as to what action to take about the Spanish Navy. The debate gets the students emotionally involved, they play roles, and it comes alive. You should emphasise the importance of not just picturing the scenes, but envisaging the sounds and feelings as well.

It is possible to visualise in a similar way for maths. The students can visualise the volume of a sphere as the formula is given. Maths formula are, after all, only abstractions from reality.

Games

It is important to defocus the learning process and focus instead on the game to be played. Distract the conscious and you produce stress free learning.

Chorus Reading

A chorus reading - all together - is good in a language class during the initial stages. It is a safer environment than a sole reading and does not make for tension.

Charts

If there is visual material, grammar charts or maths formulae to remember, they can be put up to the students left - because we store visual images in the upper left quadrant of our minds' eye.

Figuring It Out

In a language class it is better to give some examples of sentences and then challenge the students, to figure out the implicit grammar rules for themselves.

Sketches

Acting out even a simple phrase is a big memory aid.

Activation

After you have created the primary memory for new information, via the concerts and memory maps, it is a good idea to activate that material within 36 hours at the latest. Activations probably should take up about 75% of the total teaching time with the actual concert sessions about 15% and the remaining 10% devoted to the teacher acting out the information.

Visualising Success

Every third or fourth day it helps to have the students visualising themselves using the new information successfully. In a language class, they can imagine themselves in that country, using the language fluently and hearing phrases they already know. In a mathematics class they can picture themselves solving problems easily. It works.

Internal v External Motivation

Charles Schmid emphasises the importance of students having an internal motivation - "I want to learn this" rather than an external motivation - "Someone has told me to learn this".

Internal motivation comes when the subject becomes exciting, when they can see the real advantage of knowing the new information, when they feel sympathetic towards the subject.

Big Picture Analysis

It is always easier to learn the relevance of details when you have seen the big picture. So it is a good idea to sketch out the entire course at the very beginning. The students will know where they are going. This is important for science subjects, as well as history, maths or literature.

In languages, it can be very productive to include some grammar points that you may only activate in later lessons. So the students for example, actually see the past tense used for two lessons, before they are told the specific way it is constructed. But then it will no longer be a new piece of information. It will already be familiar and it should be possible to get the students to work out the rules for constructing the tense for themselves.

This is a good way of feeding in information at the semi-conscious level, as well as the fully conscious level. It is why there seems to be a "snowball" effect towards the end of an Accelerated Learning Course. The students find everything falls into place, because they have been exposed to most of the material for some time. The material was registering, but because it had not been activated and specifically highlighted, it had not been fully learnt at the conscious level.

This is what is known as global learning. Being exposed to a lot of material, but picking out parts in a planned sequence and seeing how those parts fit into the whole. It is the way children learn between 3 and 6 years old, when the pleasure and excitement of learning is most intense.

Text

It is important, in language teaching, to have adult themes. Use a story with some suspense in it. Use scenes with plenty of possibility for sensory impressions - sounds, sights, feelings, colours.

The plot should be positive and the characters sympathetic.

Flexibility

One of the principles of the new wave of pragmatic psycho-therapists can be best summarised "If you are trying something and it doesn't work - stop and try something new." The same thing applies to teaching. Watch for the feedback, the response, from your students and adapt.

Conclusion

Accelerated Learning works because it adapts the presentation of knowledge to the way people's minds really work. It does not try to adapt people to the material.

Note

1) Charles Schmid can be contacted at the LIND Institute,
   P.O. Box 14487 San Francisco C.A.

2) Further books that teachers might be interested to read can be found in the Bibliography. In addition, there are a number of books that specifically contain instructions, games and exercises to promote better utilisation of global, intuitive thinking and more ready use of imagery in creative thinking.

They include "Put your Mother on the Ceiling" (de Mille 1981), "Experiences in Visual Thinking" (McKim 1972) "Drawing on the Right Side of the Brain" (Edwards 1979) and "The Metamorphic Mind" (Samples 1976).

APPENDIX A

The Paradise Unified School Project

The following is a reprint of the official report commissioned by California State Educational Authority.

1. Summary

Accelerated Learning potential is a ESEA Title IV-C Project in its second year of state administered funding. Accelerated Learning techniques have been shown in this project to dramatically increase student learning rates in reading, maths, spelling and writing. These same strategies have improved student behaviour and time on task, while they increased teacher confidence and stress regulation in the classroom.

This project has synthesised recent research discoveries about the human mind in order to develop an instructional methodology maximally applicable to the public schools and similar private schools settings. A criterion referenced in-service programme and classroom implementation strategy has evolved from the application of this research.

Methodology

The following strategies are sequenced and systemised for application in the classroom:

1. Arousal Level - creating the optimal physiological arousal level for learning through relaxation, physical exercise, and teacher behaviour.
2. Imagery - utilising mental representatives to insure initial learning, promote retention and increase positive behaviour.
3. Teacher language - conveying high expectations for student achievement through positive suggestions, and both verbal and non verbal teacher language.
4. Music - adjusting classroom atmosphere through the systematic use of varied musical styles.
5. Complete Instructional Format - teaching material to be retained through a modification of the concert instruction originated by Dr. Lozanov.
6. Consolidation Time - guiding the absorption of new concepts and understanding.

V. Project Statistics
1981-82 Grant amount - $64,843.
Students involved: 312 experimental, 156 control
Teachers involved: 13 experimental, 6 control
1982-83 Grant amount - $51,874.
Students involved: 538 experimental, 517 control
Teachers involved: 20 experimental, 12 control

Total involved in experimental classrooms:
850 students
33 teachers:
2 Resource Specialist classrooms
3 Special Day Classes for
Learning Handicapped
1 Speech and Language therapy
program.

VI. Project Evaluation - Objective
Summary of First-Year Results:
On standardised teaching with the California Achievement Test, project students averaged a much higher gain (x + 46.88) than did control students (x + 33.42). This is a high significant effect (P <01). Excepting one, project teachers all showed gains exceeding those of the corresponding control group, gaining over 1½ times as much as control classes.

Behavioural data indicated a significant reduction in behavioural referrals for the project teachers, compared to an increase in behavioural referrals for control teachers. This was coupled with a significantly greater increase in positive ratings of student behaviour by project teachers than control teachers. Further, project teachers increased in their ability to self-regulate their stress and control classroom problems, while control teachers decreased.

Summary of Second-Year Results:
California Achievement Test administered in reading and math demonstrated again significant increases in academic learning for

project classrooms (x + 43.23). These gains were idiosyncratic to each teacher, and in some cases, students gained up to nearly twice as much in Accelerated Learning classrooms. In addition, holistically scored composition tests demonstrated significant improvement in writing and composition for students in project classes.

Behavioural data again showed Accelerated Learning methods significantly reduced behavioural problems, decreased the incidence of maladaptive behaviours and effectively improved time on task in the classroom. Finally, project teachers continued to demonstrate high levels of confidence, self regulation and classroom control.

All project data was analysed and interpreted by *Grant Evaluation and Research,* an independent grant evaluation firm in Chico, California. Their final comment, based on the two-year evaluation, was: "Given the alternative of standard classroom teaching, Accelerated Learning techniques have the potential for dramatically improving the quality of education of regular students in our classroom".

VII Subjective Project Evaluation

Teacher, student and parent response to the implementation of this project has been positive. Among the teacher comments:

1. "This project gives me an opportunity to change and learn new skills so that I may continue longer and more effectively in my teaching profession."
2. "Just like the students, I'm improving myself as a learner and thinker and person. I intend this year to release myself from some of the limitations, I've placed on my own potential."
3. "My students are gaining basic skills more quickly than ever. They're also improving their personally responsible behaviour."
4. "I was ready for a turning point in my teaching career and I feel that this has been it."
5. "I have been teaching for over 15 years. I believe that the system brings together that which we know works in a classroom."

Students comments include:

1. "I'm learning how to learn. That's important." (aged 10)
2. "Accelerated Learning helps me control myself, helps me understand things better." (aged 9)
3. "Accelerated Learning Programme helps me to do better in my work, before I begin, I concentrate on what I am going to do." (aged 9)
4. "The Accelerated Learning has given me faith in myself." (aged 9)
5. "I like to do Accelerated Learning because when I feel that I can't do something, I find out I can do it. My brain thinks I can and it relaxes and *I learn that I can learn*." (aged 10)

The objective as well as the subjective evaluations of this project clearly indicate the positive impact of this project on teachers and students.

APPENDIX B

The Pre-Recorded Language Courses

Accelerated Learning Courses are available in French, German, Spanish, Italian and English as a Foreign Language. These notes are intended to aid those readers interested in acquiring the complete courses.

The Designers

When we decided to record and print complete language courses in the five main languages we went to the leading linguistic experts in each language. All had produced at least one complete language course and many had prepared courses for the B.B.C. - now one of the leading language publishers in the world.

We approached them with some diffidence. Although we had the evidence that Accelerated Learning works at least three times more effectively than conventional teaching, we were, after all, effectively going to challenge many of their previous assumptions.

It is a tribute to their open-mindedness, and to the persuasive logic behind Accelerated Learning, that they have all embraced the new principles with whole-hearted enthusiasm. Indeed very many of the successful activations are their original creations.

The English as a Foreign Language Course has been designed by Mark Fletcher M.A. and will shortly be available for Native Speakers in German, Spanish, Portuguese, Japanese, French and several Middle to Far East Languages.

Thanks to the E.E.C.!

If we were lucky in finding the leading Course Designers, we were extremely lucky in our timing for the publication of the Accelerated Learning Language Course.

The Council of Europe has devoted many thousands of hours to a very comprehensive study that analyses the foreign language needs of the citizens of the European Economic Community.

In two major publications "The Threshold Level for Modern Language Learning by Adults" and "Waystage", they have been able to define the specific vocabulary that is needed for practical communication. The "Waystage" series, prepared by J.A. Van Ek and his colleagues, identifies all the circumstances in which a traveller, businessman or visitor would expect to find her or himself. It also identifies the most common ways in which people will want to express themselves, their opinions, their attitudes and their needs.

In a literal sense the Waystage series is an inventory of the real life practical language you would need to be able to communicate freely. We have fully incorporated all their recommendations.

The Waystage series was only published in the late 70's. Because it takes a long time to revise existing conventional language courses, it means that not only is the technique in the Accelerated Learning Language Courses novel, but the content is based on the most up to date and comprehensive research available. The pre-recorded Accelerated Learning Language Courses aim to teach a 2000 words vocabulary. This is good enough to understand 90% of a normal conversation or text.

The Differences

An Accelerated Learning Course and a Conventional Language Course are quite different. You've already seen the format for yourself.

There are some other points of difference that are not quite so obvious, however. In listing them the sublety of the technique will become apparent - and that will aid you in preparing your own course in your own specialist subject or interest.

1) While conventional language courses start out easy and get difficult, the number of words in our first lesson is virtually the same as the last lesson. You encounter from the very first scene the normal structure of the language. This is what's called "Global Learning".

The way material is presented is vital. When a small amount of information, fragmented from the whole, is presented slowly, bit by bit, and with a lot of repetition, it suggests that the material is going to be difficult. The same material presented as something one can pick up immediately, in its full complexity, suggests that one can learn it quickly and without struggle.

Yet, because Accelerated Learning presents material in a way that is so easily absorbed, you should be able to learn the text in Lesson One as easily as anything you've ever learned before. Since the first lesson will be as comprehensive as any other lesson, everything that follows it will get progressively easier. Moreover, as you progress you will find that you already know an increasingly large percentage of the material. Your rate of learning speeds up as a consequence, and so does your confidence. You will then acquire the confidence to make mistakes - because "the more mistakes you make the more chances you take". Once you lose your fear of mistakes you will achieve yet another boost in learning speed.

2) The way the course is constructed, you can't "fall behind because you missed a lesson". The structure of the language is embedded in *all* the lessons, and because you largely figure it out for yourself, if you haven't worked it out in Chapter 1, you can do so in Chapter 3. It's a global, holographic, not a linear approach. You are introduced to all the important elements straight away.

3) We aim that the Accelerated Learning Course never seems like work, it should seem like fun. It's a joyful experience. This is because the pleasure of making contact with another culture is really quite intense if it proceeds easily and quickly.

227

We have noticed that once people start learning the language by the Accelerated Learning method, they often have to force themselves to stop - as if they were reading a good book they couldn't put down.

Get past your first brief period of adjustment to this new method and you'll have the time of your life. You will genuinely *want* to learn new languages - just for the pleasure of it.

4) Initially some people do get frustrated, because they feel that they cannot be learning. If it is easy, they must be cheating! Yet all our research has shown that they remember what they learn by this method much better than they would if they focussed their attention completely on the learning task and "studied hard". Effort, in the sense of grim determination, doesn't equate with results in learning! But the Calvinist attitude dies hard!

5) We use rounded characters with whom you can become involved. There are plenty of imaginative, colourful scenes which encourage visualisation and take your mind off the act of learning.

Furthermore the conversations are not stilted, but represent real communications between people in situations that are important to them. This way you learn the meaning of words, not from rote drill, but from the *context* of the story, as you get carried along with the fun of it. It is no accident that Ionesco, the playright, developed the "Theatre of the Absurd" after reading the stilted language of an old fashioned language course.

Here's a full list of differences between and Accelerated and a Conventional course. They will suggest to you the principles you need to incorporate when you prepare your own Accelerated course.

A Summary of how a Home Accelerated Learning Course compares with a Conventional Study Course

Conventional Learning	Accelerated Learning
1. Fragmented units	1. Global units, unified text
2. Standard textbook illustrations	2. Memory Maps to bring the language in a highly visual and, therefore, memorable form

3. Flat Characters	3. Rounded Characters
4. Little emotional impact or arousal	4. Good emotional impact and arousal
5. Emphasis on phrase book learning	5. Emphasis on real communication
6. Emphasis on translation	6. Emphasis on spontaneous response
7. Early presentation of large grammar segments	7. Grammar rules introduced when the student is ready to learn them
8. Rote learning of grammar	8. Grammar taught in easy to remember and pleasurable format
9. Spoken slowly	9. Language spoken at normal rhythm
10. Based on the assumption that learning is difficult	10. Based on the fact that people learn quickly when blocks are removed
11. No concert sessions	11. Concert sessions
12. Everyday experience normally presented in straight forward format	12. Everyday experience presented in imaginative format that stimulates visualisation
13. Frequent repetition with emphasis on rote learning	13. Little repetition
14. Gives the suggestion "Keep at it . . . don't be ambitious"	14. Gives suggestion that learning is easy and fast and backs that up with proof
15. Can take one year to learn 1000-2000 words	15. Can be learned in 75 hours
16. Creates tension in learner because of need to remember	16. All necessary knowledge is in a stress free presentation
17. No peripheral stimuli	17. Lots of peripheral stimuli
18. Stress on Auditory Learning and reading	18. Comprehensive use of all learning styles

APPENDIX C

Some Current Accelerated Learning Projects

We tried to 'audit' the extent of Accelerated Learning and can report that just some of the Accelerated Learning projects now in progress and their applications are:-

San Jose State University, California (Psychology Dept. - Method Research)

University of Toronto, Ontario (Method Research)

University of Massachusetts (Dr Macrae Dhority - Stroke Patient Rehabilitation)

Louisianna State University, Alexandria (Dr Patsy Barber - Management/Shorthand)

La Verne College, California (German)

University of Houston, Texas (Arabic, Chinese, German, French, Japanese, Portuguese and Spanish)

Centre for Applied Linguistics, Arlington, Virginia (Method Research)

Murdock University, Australia

University of Adelaide, S. Australia (Dr Sigrid Gassner Roberts - German)

Colorado State University, Fort Collins (German)

Marylhurst College, Portland, Oregon (Management Degree Course, Sociology Psychology)

Lozanov Institute, Silver Springs, Maryland (teaching all main languages, plus maths and creative innovation)

Oy Yleisradio AB (Finnish Radio/T.V. station)

Breckinbridge Public Elementary School (remedial reading course for primary age children)

Iowa State University (Spanish and general method)

Lycee Voltaire School, Paris (English)

Ecole Française de Suggestopaedia, Paris (English and Russian)

Rutgers University, N.J. (Languages and Method)

University of California (Mathematics/Method/Languages)

University of Tubingen, Germany

Perdowsi University, Iran

Uppsala University, Sweden (Languages and Typing)
University of Leipzig
Institute of Intensive Language Study, Berlin
Maurice Therez Foreign Language Institute, Moscow

BIBLIOGRAPHY

ASHER J.	The strategy of the total physical response: an application of learning Russian. IRAL 3:292:299	1965
ATKINSON R.C. & SHIFFRIN R.M.	Human memory: a proposed system and its central processes. K.W. and J.T. Spence (Eds) The Psychology of Learning and Motivation Vol.II New York Academic Press	1968
BADDELEY A.D.	Short term memory for word sequences as a function of acoustic, semantic and formal similarity. Quarterly Journal of Experimental Psychology	1966
BAILEY L.G.	Observing Foreign Language Teaching. A new method for Teachers, Researchers and Supervisors. Foreign Language Annals 10/6 641-648	1977
BANCROFT W.J.	The Lozanov Method and its American adaptions Modern Language Journal 167-175	1978
BANCROFT W.J.	Language and music. Suggestopaedia and the Suzuki Method. Journal of the Society for Accelerated Learning and Teaching 3-18	1981
BANCROFT W.J.	Suggestology and Suggestopaedia. The Theory of the Lozanov Method. Journal of S.A.L.T. Vol.1 No.3	1976
BANDLER Richard GRINDER John	Frogs into Princes. Real People Press. U.S.A.	1979
BARZAKOV.I.	Optima learning: Orchestrating the best performance Brain/Mind Bulletin 1-2	1982
BLAIR Lawrence	Rhythms of Vision Warren Books N.Y.	1976
BLAIR R.	Innovative Approaches to Language Teaching Rowley Mass, Newbury House	1982
BOGEN J.E. DEZARE R.	The other side of the brain. The Bulletin of the Los	

TENHOUTEN W.D. & MARSH J.F. BORDON R & SCHUSTER D.	Angeles Neurological Societies 41 87 90 The effects of Suggestion, synchronized breathing and orchestrated music on the acquisition and retention of Spanish words. Journal of Suggestive Accelerated Learning and Teaching 1(1) 27-40	1976 1976
BRADSHAW J. NETTLETON N.	The nature of hemispheric specialisation in man. Behaviour and Brain Science 4 51-91	1981
BRANSFORD J.D. BARCLAY J.R. & FRANKS J.J.	Sentence memory: Cognitive Psychology 3(2) 193-209	1972
BROWN R. McNEILL D.	The 'Tip of the Tongue' Phenomenon. Journal of Verbal Learning and Verbal Behaviour 5(4) 325-37	1966
BUDZYNSKI T.	Biofeedback and the twilight state of consciousness. Consciousness and Self Regulation Vol.1. Advances in research G.E. Schwartz and D. Shapiro eds New York Pieum Press	1976
BUZAN Tony	Use Your Head. Ariel Books. B.B.C. Publications	1980
CASKEY O. & FLAKE M.	Suggestive Accelerated Learning. Adaptations of the Lozanov Method. Texas Tech University	1976
CHAFE W.L.	Language and memory. Language 49 261-281	1973
CLEVELAND Bernard F.	Master Teaching. Connecting Link Press 574 W 20850 Field Drive, Muskego W1 53150	1982
COLLINS A.M. Quillan M.R.	Retrieval time from semantic memory Journal of Verbal Learning and Verbal Behaviour 8;240-71	1969
CURRAN C.	Counseling Learning. A Whole Person Model of Education. New York: Grune and Stratton	1972
CURRAN C.	Counseling learning in second languages Apple River Press	1976

CURRAN E.A.	NIE An agenda for the 80s. Educational Researcher 11 (5) 10-12-21	1981
DAVIDSON D.	Current approaches in the teaching of grammar. ESL Language in Education: Theory and Practice 5 Arlington V.A. Center for Applied Linguistics	1978
deMILLE R.	Put your mother on the ceiling: Santa Barbara CA Ross Erikson	1981
DILTS R.	Neuro Linguistic Programming. Meta Publications	1979
DIMOND S.	Neuropsychology. A textbook of systems and psychological functions of the human brain London Butterworths	1979
DIAGRAM GROUP	The Brain users Manual. Berkeley Books N.Y.	1981
ECCLES J.	Evaluation of the brain in relation to the development of the self-conscious mind Annals of the New York Academy of Science 299 161-179	1977
EDWARDS B.	Drawing on the right side of the brain. A course in enhancing creativity and artistic confidence Los Angeles J.P. Tarcher	1979
EK van J.A.	Threshold level for Modern Language Learning Council of Europe	1980
ERICKSON Milton	The Collected Papers of Milton H. Erickson on Hypnosis. N.Y. Irvington Publ.	1980
FERGUSON M.	The Brain Revolution. London David Poynter	1974
FERGUSON M.	The Aquarian conspiracy. Personal growth and social transformation in the 1980's Los Angeles J.P. Tarcher	1980
FERGUSON M.	The Brain/Mind Bulletin. Interface Press PO Box 42211 4717 N. Figuero St. L.A. CA90042	
FOX P.	Reading as a whole brain function. The Reading Teacher 33.7-14	1979
GALYEAN B.C.	Guided imagery aids in writing	

	skills of tenth graders. Association for Humanistic Psychology Newsletter 7	1982
GALYEAN B.C.	Human teaching and human learning in the language class. Confluent teaching strategies applied to language teaching. Santa Barbara CA Cedarc	1976
GATTEGNO C.	The common sense of teaching foreign language New York Educational Solutions second edition	1976
GAWAIN Shakti	Creative Visualization. Whatever Publishing Inc. PO Box 137 Mill Valley California CA94941	
GAZZANIGA M.S. & le DOUX J.	The Integrated Mind. New York Plenium Press	1978
GAZZANIGA M.S.	The bisected brain. Appleton Century Crofts	1970
GESCHWIND N.	The organization of language and the brain Science 170 940-944	1970
GUIORA A.Z. HARLAN L. LANE L.A. BOSWORTH	An exploration of some personality variables in authentic pronunciation of a second language. In H. Lane and E. Zale (eds) Studies in Language and Language Behaviour Ann Arbor: University of Michigan	1967
HARDY A & MERSHON B.	Field based vs traditional teacher education. A study of learning style preference. The teacher Educator 16 23-26	1980-81
HILL Jane H.	Foreign accents. Language acquisition and cerebal dominance revisited. Language Learning 20 237 248	1970
HOLDEN C.	Paul MacLean and the triune brain. Science 204 1066-1068	1979
HOUSTON Jean	The Possible Human. A course in Enhancing your Physical, Mental and Creative Abilities. J.P. Tarcher Los Angeles	1982
JAKOBIVITS L.A.	Foreign Language Learning. A Pyscholinguistic Analysis of the Issues Rowley Mass Newbury	1970a

KAGAN J.,   House Psychological significance of
MOSS H.A. &   styles of conceptualization
SIGEL I.E.   Basic cognitive
WRIGHT J.C. &   processes in children.
KAGAN J. (Eds).   Monographs of the Society for
                   Research in Child Development
                   28 73-112   1963

KEY Wilson   Subliminal Seduction   New
Bryan   American Library N.Y.   1978
KINSBOURNE M.   Hemispheric specialization and
                   the growth in short term
                   understanding. American
                   Psychologist 37 411-420   1982
KINTSCH W &   Homophones and synonyms
BUSCHKE H.   in short term memory. Journal of
                   Experimental Psychology   1969
KLEINBERG J. &   Constancy in STM bits and chunks.
H. KAUFMAN   J Exp Psycho 90 326-333   1971

KLINE P.   The Sandy Springs Experiment.
                   Applying Relaxation Techniques to
                   Education. Journal of SALT
                   Vol.1 No.1   1976
KNIBBLER W.   A closer look at
                   Suggestopaedia and the Silent Way.
                   Journal of the Society for
                   Accelerated Learning and Teaching
                   7/4   1984
KOLB David   Experimental Learning. Experience
                   as the source of Learning and
                   Development. Prentice Hall,
                   Englewood Cliffs, New Jersey 07632   1983
KRASHEN S.   The Natural Approach. Language
TERRELL T.   Acquisition   Pergamon Press Oxford   1983

KRIPPNER S.   Human possibilities. Mind
                   research in the USSR and Eastern
                   Europe. Garden City N.Y.
                   Anchor Books   1980
LADO R.   Memory span as a factor
                   in second language learning
                   IRAL 3 123 130   1965
LANKTON S.R.   Practical Magic   Meta Publ. Box 565
                   Cupertino California 95014
LANKTON S. &   The Answer Within. A clinical
LANKTON C.   Framework of Erickson

236

	Hypnotherapy N.Y. Brunner/Mazel	1983
LORAGNE H.	The Memory Book. Star Book.	
LUCAS J.	Wyndham Publ.	
LOZANOV G.	Suggestology and Outlines of Suggestopedy New York. Gordon and Breach	1978
LOZANOV G. & BALEVSKY P.	The Effect of the Suggestopaedic System of instruction on the Physical Development State of Health and Working Capacity of First and Second Grade Pupils. Suggestology and Suggestopaedia Vol.1 No.3	1975
LUBORSHY L.	Introduction to the fifth edition of D. Rappaport Emotions and Memory New York International Universities Press	1971
LURIA A.R.	The Mind of a Mnemonist. New York Basic Books	1968
McCARTHY Bernice	The 4 Mat System. Teaching to Learning Styles with Right/Left mode Techniques Excel Inco 600 Enterprise DR Suite 101 Oak Brook IL 60521	
McLUHAN Marshall	Understanding Media The Extension of Man New York MacGraw Hill	1964
MACHADO Dr Luiz	Emotology and Emotopedia Rio de Janeiro	1984
MALIN D.H. &	Synthetic rat scotophobin induces dark avoidance in mice Science 1219 1220	1972
MANDLER G.	Organization and memory. In K.W. Spence and J.T. Spence (eds) The Psychology of learning and motivation New York Academic Press	1967
MARINO Raul	Fisiologia das Emocoes (Physiology of Emotions)	1975
MASLOW A.H.	Motivation and Personality (2nd Edition) New York Harper and Row	1970
MELTON A.W.	Implications of short term memory for a general theory of memory. J Verb Learn Verb Behav	1963
MELTON A.W.	The concept of coding in	

	learning memory theory Memory and Cognition 1 508-12	1973
METHUEUS	Manual of Psychology. Readings in Human Memory Methuen Ltd.	
MIELE Philip	Suggestopedia Utopia Unlimited Publishers U.S.A.	1981
MIELE Philip	The Power of Suggestion. A new way of learning Languages Parade Mag.12	1978
MILLER G.A.	The magical number sevenplus of minus two. Some limits on our capacity for processing information Psychological review 63 81 97	1956
MILLER Sue	The Wholemind Works. Creative Ideas for Doing it all P.O. Box 527 Gresham Oregon 97030	
MILLER George	Human Memory and the Storage of Information Transactions of Information Theory IT2 129 137	1956
MILNER Brenda	Memory and the medial temporal regions of the brain. In Pribram and Broadbent 29-50	1970
MODIGHAMI V. & SEAMON G.	Transfer of information from short to long term memory J Exp Psych 102 768 772	1974
MOSKOWITZ Gertrude	The effects of training foreign language teachers. Interaction Analysis Foreign Language Annals. 1 218-235	1968
NAIMAN N. FROHLICH M. STERN H. TODESCO A.	The Good Language Learner. Research in Education. Series 7 Toronto The Ontario Institute for Studies in Education	1978
NEWMAN E.	The Creative Construction. Theory of Second Language acquisition and its implications for language teaching Modern Languages LX1/4	1980
ORNSTEIN Robert	The Education of the Intuitive Mode. The Psychology of Consciousness. London, Harcourt Brace	1977
PAIVIO A.	Mental imagery in associative learning and memory Psychological Review 76 241-263	1969

PAVLIDIS G.	Do eye movements hold the key to dyslexia Neuropsychologia 19 57 64	1980
PERLS Frederick S.	Gestalt Therapy Verbatim Utah Real People Press	1969
PETERS Thomas J. & WATERMAN Robert H. Jr.	In Search of Excellence Lessons from America's Best run Companies Harper and Row New York	1982
POPE K. & SINGER J.L.	The stream of consciousness Scientific investigations into the flow of human experience New York Plenum Press	1978
PRIBRAM K.H. BROADBENT D.E.	Biology of Memory New York Academic Press	1970
RAPPAPORT D.A.	Emotions and Memory. Fifth edition New York International Universities Press	1971
RICO Gabriele Lusser	Writing in the Natural Way. Using Right Brain Techniques to Release your Expressive Powers J.P. Tarcher Inc. Los Angeles	1983
RIVERS Wilga M.	The Psychologist and the Foreign Language Teacher Chicago Univ. of Chicago	1964
RUSSELL Peter	The Brain Book. Rautledge and Kegan Paul London	1980
SAFARIS F.	Une revolution dans l'art d'apprendre Paris Laffont	1978
SAMPLES Bob	The Metaphoric Mind	1976
SAMPLES Bob CHARLES Cheryl & BARNHARDT D.	The Whole School Book; Teaching and Learning in the 20th Century	1977
SAMUELS M. & SAMUELS N.	Seeing with the mind's eye. The history, techniques and uses of visualization. New York Random House, Bookworks	1975
SATIR Virginia	Peoplemaking Palo Alto CA Science and Behaviour Books Inc.	1972
SCHUSTER D.	A preliminary evaluation of the suggestive accelerative Lozanov method in teaching	

	beginning Spanish Journal of Suggestive Accelerative Learning and Teaching 1 41-47	1976
SHIFFRIN R.M.	Memory search. Chapter 12 in Norman D.A. (ed) Models of Human Memory 375-447	1970
SIMARTON O. Carl MD	Getting Well Again St Martins Press New York	
SHULMAN H.G.	Encoding and retention of semantic and phonemic information in short term memory. Journal of Verbal Learning and verbal behaviour	1970
SPRINGER S.P. & DEUTSCH G.	Left Brain, Right Brain San Franscisco W.H. Freeman	1981
STARR W.	The Suzuki Violinist. Knoxville Kingston Ellis Press	1976
STEVICK E.	A Way and Ways. Rowley Mass Newbury House	1980
STEVICK E.	Memory, Meaning and Method. Some Psychological Perspectives on Language Learning. Rowley Mass Newbury House	1976
TOMATIS A.	Education et Dyslexic 3rd ed Paris Editions ESF	1978
TORRANCE E.P. & MYERS R.E.	Creative Learning and Teaching. New York Harper and Row	1970
TULVING E.	The effect of alphabetical subjective organisation on memorizing unrelated words. Canadian J of Psych 16 185-191	1962
TULVING E. & OSLER S.	Effectiveness of retrieval cues in memory for words. Journal of Experimental Psychology.	1968
UNDERWOOD B.J.	Attributes of memory. Psychological Review 76 559 73	1969
WATSON LYALL	Supernature Hodder and Stoughton London	1979
WAUGH N.C.	Immediate memory as a function of repetition Journal of Verbal Learning and Verbal Behaviour	1963
WENGER Win	How to increase your intelligence.	1980
WICKENS D.D.	Encoding categories of words, an empirical approach to meaning. Psychological Review.	1970

240

INDEX

Active Concert 89,206,207,211,213
Adams, M.J. 60
Air Force Research Laboratories, Bedford, Mass. 50
Aitken, Professor 66
Albinoni 88
Alpha Brain Waves 13,22-24,27,81,90,103,104,114,166,183,185
American Society for Training & Development 83
Annamalai University, India 98
Applegate, Roy 118
Applied Psychology Unit, Cambridge 60
ARAMCO 120
Aristotle 97,129
Aserinsky, Eugene 49
Asher, V.N. 171
A. T. & T. 120
Athens 97
Awareness Relaxation 178,179,183

Bach 20,88,98,103,108,123
Bacon, Francis 130
Baddeley, Dr. A. 29,30,48,60
Bancroft, Jane 125
Bandler, Richard 152,162
Bannister, Dr. Roger 82
Baroque Music 88,89,100,102-104,169,187,193,202,205,208,212
Barzakov Institute 120
Barzakov, Ivan 121,122,125
Bassin 50
Bauer 55
Bayer College of Medicine 31
B.B.C. 60,225
Beck, Robert 104
Beeby, Valerie 129,163
Beecher, Dr. 79
Beethoven 97,99
Belanger, Mme. 102
Bell Laboratories 69
Bell Telephones 120
Berlitz 112
Bernstein 151
Beta Brain Waves 13,22-24,27,87,104,114
Biofeedback 25,80,86,89,103
Biofeedback Centre, Denver 25
Bogen, Joseph 16
Bohemianism 131
Bonny 105
Bowen 171
Bower, Gordon 44,65

Bradshaw 106
Brahms 99
Brain Scans 14,106,107
Brain Stem 18
Bransford, John 46,172
Brierly, J.B. 177
British Medical Council 17
Broca's Area 9
Bruner, Dr. Jerome 25,89
Budzynski, Dr. Thomas 53,65
Buzan, Tony

California Institute of Technology 11
California State Educational Authority 222
California State University 118
Cambridge University 50
Carroll 31
Caycedo, Alfonso 145
C.B.C. 143
Centre for Applied Linguistics 125
Cerebellum 18
Cerebral Cortex 20
Cheureul, Dr. 6
Chicago 2
Chladni, Ernest 100,108
Cicero 60,74
Cleveland, Bernard, F. 162
Confucius 97
Cooter, Stephen 103,105,129
Copernicus 218
Corelli 88,103
Corpus Callosum 11,12,16,25,27
Council of Europe 226
Cristofoli, Vibeka 122
Craik, J. 46,171
Crick 8
Curran, C.A. 171
Curreau, Jean 122

da Vinci 15,130
Defence Dept. 120
de Lacoste Utamsing, Dr. Christine 15
Delta Airlines 120
Delta Brain Waves 22-24,27
Dekerian, Debra 60
de Mille 221
Department of Commerce 120
Dewan, Dr. Edmond 50
Dilts 152
Dimond, Stuart 16

Doman, Glenn 209
Durovy, Patricia 83

Ebbinghaus, Hermann 35,37,38,113,138
Ecole Francaise de Suggestopedie 123
Edinburgh Hospital 51
Edinburgh University 66
Edwards, B. 221
E.E.C. 226
Eidetic Images 69
Eidetic Memory 48
Einstein 15,20,218
Eliot, T.S. 130
Encode 31
Encoding 45
Epictetus 122
Epstein, H.T. 9
Erickson, Milton 162
Evans, Chris 49,50,52,70
Evans, Peter 49

Finnish Government 2
Fletcher, Mark 226
Flood 31
Fresno 172
Freud 62

Galin 105
Gallileo 218
Gallwey, Tim 77,78
Garfield, Patricia 51
Gattengno, Caleb 172
General Motors 2,120
Glanzer 44
Glueck, Dr. Bernard 16
Godden, Dr. Duncan 48
Green, Dr. Alyce 80
Green, Dr. Elmer 80
Grinder, John 152,162
Gritton, Charles 118
Guiora, Professor A.Z. 173

Haber, Ralph 62
Halici, Mehmed Ali 66
Halpern, Stephen 101
Handel 101,103,106
Hardy, C.A. 106
Harvard University 9,57,79,151
Hatch, Dr. Donald 101

Haydn 20,88,99
Herder 10
Hilton Hotels 2,120
Holistic Learning 52,91,147
Hollander, Paul 121,125,150,152
Houston, ... Dr. Jean 3
Houston University 121
Howe, Elias 51,55
Humphrey, Dr. 177
Humphrey, Nicholas 50
Hypermnesia 67,73,87,113
Hypopaedia 52
Hypothalamus 18,178

IBM 125,152
Idzikowsky, Dr. Chris 51
Iliad 97
Imagination and Suggestion 84
Institute for Consciousness and Music, Baltimore 104
Institute for Living, Hartford 16
Ionosphere 104
Iowa State University 2,84,117,125,216
I.Q. 19,22,26,76,114,142

Jaensch, E.R. 67
Jarvik 31
Jenny, Dr. Hans 100,101,102
Jensen, Dr. Bernard 97

Kaplan, Lester 129,172
Katholieke University 125
Kaumatara, Chief 67
Kayserling, Count 98
Kelvin, Lord 21
Kennedy, J.F. 63
Key, Professor Wilson Bryan 69,70,140
Kinaesthetic 62,152,154,159,160,161,164,169,194,195,214,217
Kintsch, K. 44,171
Kleinsmith 172
Kleitman, N. 49
Kline, Peter 87-94,149
Knibbler, Wil 125
Koestler, Arthur 10,24
Koltanovski 46
Krashen, Stephen 170,199,200

Landahl, Christer 125
Landseer, Sir Edwin 15
Lawlor, Michael 125
Lawrence, Ruth 22

Lecky, Prescott 82
Lehman College 142
Lenin Institute, Moscow 115,129
Limbic System 18,19,27,179,194
LIND Institute 121,217
Lindsay, H.R. 63,65
Linton, Mangold 54
Locke, John 48
London University 102
Long Term Memory 29,31-34,36,39,53,174
Louisiana State University 121
Lozanov, Georgi 2,84,85,87,88,90,91,93,95,96,102,104,111-114,118,120,
            121,122,126,132,133,138,142,145,147,149,187,222
Lozanov Learning Institute, Silver Spring 118,120,125
Lozanov Institute, Verduz 122,125
Lozanov Learning Institute, Washington 84,87,139
Luria, Professor 70
Lycee Voltaire School 122

Mabry, Mrs Jean 83
Machado, Luiz 19,125
McCarthy, Bernice 161
McConnell, J.V. 31
McGill University 67
McKim 221
Maclean, Dr. Paul 17,106
McLuhan, Marshall 83
McWhirter, Norris 82
Mammalian Brain 18
Manners, ... Dr. 101
Massachusetts Institute of Technology 69
Mehrabian, Robert 151
Meinzer 44
Memory Maps 26-27,39,55,65,74,86,96,108-109,129,147,164,168,
            174-175,185,191,192,195,201,206-207,211,219
Mendelsohn 103
Menninger Clinic 80-81
Mental Maps 88,211
Merek, Stephanie 103
Meta Learning 163
Mezzofani, Cardinal 67
Michelangelo 20
Michigan State University 21
Miele, Philip 134
Miller, George 57,58
Milton, John 97
Mind Maps 65
Monthie, Judith 123
Morrison, Alex 79
Motor Cortex 67

Mozart 102,108,123
Murdoch 35

Napoleon 77
Nationalized Thompson Electronics Company 123
Neo-Cortex 18,27
Nettleman 106
Neuroblasts 5
Neuro-Linguistic Programming 152
Neurons 22,26,69
New York University, Dept. of Psychology 76
Nickerson, R.S. 60,62
Niclaus, Jack 77
Nitsch, K.E. 57
Norman, D.A. 30,63,65
Northwest University 137

O'Connell, Peter 124,125,173
Oppenheimer 218
Optima Learning Institute 125
Ornstein, Robert 2,11,13
Ostrander, Sheila 85
Ottawa University 99
Oxford University 22

Panathenes 97
Paradise School 118-121,129,222
Passive Concert 206,208,211,213
Penfield, Dr. Wilder 67,73
Peterson, Dr. E. 118
Phelps, Professor Michael 107
Pieron, Henry 52
Placebo 79
Plato 7
Pollock, Cecelia 142-143
Prall, Robert 125
Presley, Elvis 63
Primacy 41,42,53,167
Pritchard, Allyn 118
Project Renaissance 121
Pythagoras 97,104,108-109

Queen Elizabeth 219

Rabcsak, M. 116
Random Access Memory (RAM) 29
Rand, Pamela 121
Random Dot 69
Rapid Eye Movement (REM) 49-51,114-115
Rappaport, D.A. 19

Read Only Memory (ROM) 30
Reber, A.S. 46
Recency 41-42,53-54,167
Receptive Concert 89
Rembrandt 20
Reptilian Brain 18,27
Renaissance Man 130
Rettallack, Mrs 99,108
Rig Veda 66
R.N.A. 20,31,39
Rosenthal, Dr. 76
Rosenweig, Mark 20
Ross 120
Russell, Bertrand 20
Russell, Peter 53,71

S 70
Safaris, Fanny 123,125
SALT 117,125,129,216
Samuels, Dr. David 20
Samples 221
Satir, Virginia 162
Saucer, K. 170
Saudi Arabian Airlines 120
Schale, Florence 137
Schatzman, Dr. Morton 51
Schliecher, Carl 94
Schmid, Charles 48,121,142,150,217-220
School of English Studies 124,125
School of Language Studies Foreign Service Institute 170-171
Schroeder, Lynn 85
Schumann Resonance 104
Schuster, Dr. Don 2,117,118,125,129,216
Schwartz, Jack 9
Scotophobin 32,39
SEAL 216
Seligen, H.W. 173
Sellers, Peter 173
Sensory Systems 152
Severstsov Institute 16
Seyle, Dr. Hans 177
Shaa, Yogi 67
Shamans 98
Shankar, Ravi 99
Shaw, Bernard 20
Shell Oil 2,120,123
Shiffrin, R.N. 49
Short Term Memory 29-39,53,176
Simonides 60
Singh, Dr. 98

Smirnova, Dr. N.L. 115,129
Socrates 150
Solomon, Dr. George 178
Sophia University 111
Sperry, Roger 2,11,15,106
State Department 120
Stein, B. 106
Stellenbosch University 121
Stern, Aaron 21
Stern, Edith 21
Stevenson, Robert Louis 51
Stevick, Earl W. 170,171
Stockwell, Tony 122
Suggestion and Hypnotism 83
Summer, Lisa 104
Suggestology 145
Super Learning 84-85
Suzuki, Shinichi 143,145
Symbiosis 24,32,151
Synaesthia 70,74,86
Synapse 8

Talmud 29
Taylor, Jean 118
Telemann 88,103
Tennyson 20
Temporal Cortex 68
Terman, Dr. 22
Terrell, Tracy 199
Thalamus 18
Theta Brain Waves 22-25,27,81,103,105
Theory of Relativity 15
Tilney, Dr. Frederic 9
Tomatis, Dr. Alfred 145
Tomography 107
Tomoyori, Hideaki 66
Total Time Hypothesis 36
Toronto University 43
Totten, H.L. 106
Travis Air Force Base 80
Triune Brain 17-18,27,106
Tryptophan 6
Tulving, Endel 43,46,167,199
Twain, Mark 210

U.C.L.A. 20
U.N.E.S.C.O. 3,8,93,120,125,142
Ungar, George 31
University of Austin 121
University of California 107

University of Canada 125
University of Colorado 25
University of Montreal 177
University of Leipzig 20
University of New South Wales 177
University of North Texas 106
University of Rio de Janeiro 19,125
University of Rochester 62
University of Sophia 84,87
University of Texas 15,125
Uppsala University 122,125
U.S. Government 2,120,125
U.S. National Research Council 132

V.A.K. (Visual, Auditory, Kinaesthetic 152-164,175,206,214
Vanderbilt University 57
Van Ek, J.A. 226
Vivaldi 88,103
Von Restorff 42,62,167

Watson 8
Watson, Lyall 16
Waugh 30,35
Waystage 226
Wenger, Dr. Win 121,150-151
Weizman Institute 20
Western Language Centre 125,216
Wernicke's Area 17
Winzenz, D. 44,55
Witte, Karl 21
Wordsworth 20,184

Zaner-Bloser 152
Zeigarnick 53,167
Zeppelin, Led 102